THE REAL READER'S QUARTERLY

Slightly Foxed

'The Paris Effect'

NO.61   SPRING 2019

Editors Gail Pirkis & Hazel Wood
Marketing & publicity Stephanie Allen & Jennie Harrison Bunning
Bookshops Anna Kirk
Subscriptions Hattie Summers

Cover illustration by Faith Chevannes

Faith Chevannes is from the Tamar valley on the Devon and Cornwall border. Her drypoint prints and mixed media pieces are inspired by the spectacular landscape around her and reflect its ever-changing seasons, its wildlife and its ancient farming cycles. See her website www.faithchevannes.com or follow her on Instagram (faithchevannesart), Facebook (faith chevannes art) or Twitter (faith chevannes@faithcartist).

Design by Octavius Murray

Layout by Andrew Evans

Colophon and tailpiece by David Eccles

© The contributors 2019

Published by Slightly Foxed Limited
53 Hoxton Square
London N1 6PB

tel 020 7033 0258
email office@foxedquarterly.com
www.foxedquarterly.com

Slightly Foxed is published quarterly in early March, June, September and December

Annual subscription rates (4 issues)
UK and Ireland £48; Overseas £56

Single copies of this issue can be bought for £12.50 (UK) or £14.50 (Overseas)

All back issues in printed form are also available

ISBN 978-1-910898-25-3
ISSN 1742-5794

Printed and bound by Smith Settle, Yeadon, West Yorkshire

Contents

Contents

John Watson

The Slightly Foxed Podcast

The first four episodes of our new podcast are now available. To listen, visit www.foxedquarterly.com/pod or search for Slightly Foxed on Audioboom, iTunes or your Podcast App. Future episodes will be available on the 15th of each month.

Subscriber Benefits

Slightly Foxed can obtain any books reviewed in this issue, whether new or second-hand. To enquire about a book, to access the digital edition of *Slightly Foxed* or to view a list of membership benefits, visit www.foxedquarterly.com/members or contact the office: 020 7033 0258 / office@foxedquarterly.com.

From the Editors

As many of you will already have gathered, if only from the discreet note on the contents page of the winter issue, this spring we've embarked on a new project, the *Slightly Foxed* podcast. Your reaction to this may possibly have been the same as ours when the idea was first put to us: 'What exactly *is* a podcast?' But now that, with some very knowledgeable assistance, we've got the hang of it, we realize what an enjoyable way it is of sharing with you more of our life behind the scenes at *SF* and introducing you to some of the interesting people who help to make the magazine what it is: our varied and very individual contributors, our illustrators and designers, our printers, the independent booksellers who stock us – the list is endless. Think of it as a kind of *Slightly Foxed* on air, giving what is sometimes called 'added value'.

So from now on, on the 15th of each month, we'll be inviting you to join us round the table here in Hoxton to meet one or other of them and learn about their own particular experience and expertise, talk about books we're enjoying, and share what's going on in – and sometimes out of – the office. We do hope you'll join us, if you haven't done so already. The podcasts are completely free and the first four episodes are available to listen to now. If you enjoy them, please put the word about; and if you have any difficulty accessing them just let us know and we'll do our best to help.

One reality of life, as we're sure you all agree, is that it's not getting any cheaper, and prices are continuing to rise. In our case these include rent, paper, postage and many other essentials. We've been agonizing for some time now about how to absorb these costs without raising our subscription price, but it's six years since we last did so, and now Mark our accountant has spoken to us quite severely on the subject. So with heavy hearts we've agreed that from 1 February the price of an annual *SF* subscription will go up by £8. True, it's still only the price of a decent meal out and much longer lasting, but we do understand that for many of us these are days of uncomfortable belt-tightening. We'd be very sad to lose any of you, so we're holding a small number of subscriptions at the old price. If you are a long-term subscriber who finds the increase a step too far, please drop us a line.

More cheerfully, the latest of the Slightly Foxed Editions is a fascinating one: James (now Jan) Morris's account of the forty years he spent living as a man but utterly convinced that he was a woman – a conviction which finally led him to a gender reassignment operation in Casablanca at a time when this was relatively unheard of. A devoted husband and father of four children, James was already well known as a daring reporter and a marvellous travel writer, as well as a distinguished historian of the British Empire, and this news created a sensation. *Conundrum* however, though gripping, is anything but sensational. It's a thoughtful and moving book which casts a calm light on what is now a hotly debated issue.

Finally, many congratulations to the winner of our tenth annual crossword competition, Lorna Raynes, who receives a free annual subscription. If any of the clues defeated you, the answers are on p.93.

GAIL PIRKIS & HAZEL WOOD

The Paris Effect

LAURA FREEMAN

Brimming. That was how I spent my first weeks in Paris. Brimming with tears at the smallest setback. For Nancy Mitford's Northey in *Don't Tell Alfred*, dispatched to Paris to be secretary to Fanny Wincham, the new Madame l'Ambassadrice at the British Embassy, it is the 'cruel food' of France that sets her off. Beef consommé. Brimming. Lobster. Brimming. Foie gras. Brimming. 'A Frenchman on board told me what they do to sweet geese for pâté de foie gras,' says Northey at dinner on her first night at the Ambassador's Residence. 'Very wrong and stupid of him,' says Fanny.

I, meanwhile, brimmed at everything. Dropped Métro ticket? Wind howling down the Tuileries? ('The draughtiest place in Paris,' says Grace de Valhubert's Nanny in Mitford's *The Blessing*.) Not a *Times* or a *Telegraph* to be had in three arrondissements? ('I say – I've thought of something else – the papers are better at home,' insists Fanny).

'One's emotions are intensified in Paris,' Fabrice de Sauveterre tells Linda in *The Pursuit of Love*, 'one can be more happy and also more unhappy here than in any other place.' In those first two months of the year, I was very unhappy. Installed in a Foreign Office flat in the Marais with my diplomat fiancé Andy, I was white with homesickness. Each morning, as he left for the Embassy, I would look around our borrowed flat and it would begin. Le brimming.

Paris wasn't how I'd imagined it. I knew my Mitford. I would

Nancy Mitford's *The Pursuit of Love* (1945), *The Blessing* (1951) and *Don't Tell Alfred* (1960) are all available in paperback from Penguin at £8.99 each.

arrive, an English ugly duckling in ill-fitting clothes, speaking schoolgirl French ('*Je suis la fille d'un très important lord anglais,*' Linda tells Fabrice when he picks her up at the Gare du Nord), and reappear several weeks later a fluent, soignée swan. I would, by some Mitford miracle, become *coiffée* and *maquillée* and *parfumée* and *manicurée* and *pedicurée*. I would not stand on the Pont Neuf during the wettest January for fifty years, umbrella blown inside out, brimming tears into the Seine.

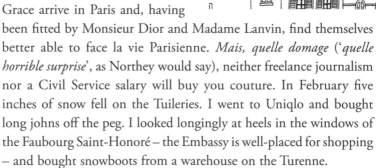

Northey, Fanny, Linda and Grace arrive in Paris and, having been fitted by Monsieur Dior and Madame Lanvin, find themselves better able to face la vie Parisienne. *Mais, quelle domage* ('*quelle horrible surprise*', as Northey would say), neither freelance journalism nor a Civil Service salary will buy you couture. In February five inches of snow fell on the Tuileries. I went to Uniqlo and bought long johns off the peg. I looked longingly at heels in the windows of the Faubourg Saint-Honoré – the Embassy is well-placed for shopping – and bought snowboots from a warehouse on the Turenne.

When I wasn't brimming or shopping for thermals, I spent whole afternoons in bed with Alfred, Fabrice and Charles-Édouard de Valhubert. Mitford knew her expat stuff. She lived and wrote in Paris for nearly thirty years. Her Fabrice was Colonel Gaston Palewski, a close ally of Charles de Gaulle. 'The publishers know they can sell any amount of books about France,' says Ambassador Alfred. 'In fact France, like Love, is a certain winner on a title page.' Nancy Mitford gave the publishers what they wanted. *The Pursuit of Love, The Blessing* and *Don't Tell Alfred* all whisk Linda, Grace and Fanny to Paris.

I started with *Don't Tell Alfred* (1960). Here was the Embassy fantasy I was supposed to be living in Andy's year-long secondment from Whitehall to Paris. 'Don't tell Alfred' is Fanny's catchphrase when the diplomatic day doesn't go to plan. When, for instance, Northey, frivolous daughter of Fanny's sensible cousin Louisa, loads a hamper of lobsters into the Embassy Rolls-Royce, drives them to Rouen and releases them. When Fanny's bearded eldest son David, now a Zen Buddhist, appears with

a Chinese babe-in-arms, evidently not his own. When Basil, her whiskered, wayward middle son, sets up camp with a party of pooped English tourists who sing 'Roll Out the Barrel' on the Embassy lawn. When her youngest son Charlie and adopted son Fabrice abscond from Eton to promote a rock star called Yanky Fonzy. When gossip columnist Amyas Mockbar devotes his daily 'Paris Page' to scurrilous reports on the failure of Alfred's mission. 'Well-informed circles are speculating on Sir Alfred's future, and rumour has it that he may shortly be posted to Rangoon . . .' Better, perhaps, not to tell Alfred, former Chair of Pastoral Theology at Oxford. Don't tell Andy, I said to myself each evening. Don't let on about another day's sniffling by the Seine.

'Mine is intended to be a serious mission,' Alfred tells Fanny after his surprise appointment. 'Sobriety, security the keynotes.' The out-going Ambassador Sir Louis Leone and Ambassadress Lady Leone (if only she *would* go) had held a 'glittering court'. Fanny, dowdy wife of a tweedy don, wonders how she will cope. 'With my absent-mindedness and ghastly food and ghastly clothes I should become the Aunt Sally of diplomatic life, a butt and a joke.'

Fanny gets the hang of it, of course, as all Mitford's heroines do. They are carried away by the beauty of the city, coffee on the breeze, chocolate profiteroles on Sèvres plates. 'I was beginning to get used to such meals,' says Fanny, 'but they always made me feel rather drunk and stupid for an hour or two afterwards.'

She is smitten with the 'honey-coloured' Embassy, the Residence and courtyard entresol, where Lady Leone, refusing to leave, barricades herself in with gramophone and champagne. The house is a haven of delight. The garden opens

> to a vista of trees; the only solid edifice in sight is the dome of the Invalides, a purple shadow on the horizon, hardly visible through summer leaves. Except for that and the Eiffel Tower, on the extreme right hand of this prospect, there is nothing to show that the house is situated in the centre of the most prosperous and busy capital on the Continent of Europe.

If you had told me when I first read *Don't Tell Alfred* aged 13 that I would one day see that house and garden, I would have rolled my eyes. It was so much the stuff of, well, novels. These things happen to other people. To bolting Lindas, not stay-at-home Lauras. It was wonderful and strange to watch the Royal Wedding on a screen in the Embassy ballroom, like falling into a set-piece chapter in a book. From the garden, where we had Pimms and quiche, you really can't see any building but the Tour Eiffel. The Embassy roses are the best in the city, all in bloom for the Queen's Birthday Party in May. The Residence, 'bought lock, stock and barrel from Napoleon's sister', is as perfect, pompous and imperial as Mitford remembers it.

Nancy Mitford was a comfort during those first brimming, homesick weeks and months. To laugh at myself, as she laughs at everyone around her, English or French, made being away more bearable. I was as resistant to the city's charms as Grace's dreary Nanny who decries the Tuileries, longs for Hyde Park and will eat only Tiptree's strawberry jam, bought from the English grocer.

One Friday night, coming back to Paris after a week in London, I sat on my suitcase at the Gare du Nord and howled, as Linda had. Linda, of course, is scooped up by Fabrice, put into a taxi and taken to luncheon. So begins their love affair. After several minutes, no Fabrice presenting himself, I pulled myself together, bought a Carnet Métro and took Ligne 4 towards the flat. Dark Frenchmen in Homburg hats are not to be counted on. Besides, Andy might have minded.

Paris will be perfect in the spring, I was promised as the February snow turned to slush. So it proved. By the time the hollyhocks were out in the Square Georges Cain, I felt less of a misfit, less homesick. On a bright day, I walked, as Fanny and Uncle Davey had, to the Rue de Saintonge. In Davey's day the Saintonge was lined with workers in morocco, gold and silver, makers of buttons, keys, ribbons, watches and wigs. Today, it is all boutiques for BoBos – the city's Bourgeois Bohemians. There is a coffee shop called La Di Da and a café, PH7 Equilibre, serving 'Buddha Bowls' according to a 'Concept Acido Basique'. At Finger in the Nose you can buy lamé bikinis for toddlers. Of the old Saintonge, only a bookbinder's survives. Looking into the windows at the marbled papers I felt for the first time in six months halfway happy and almost at home. I saw the city Mitford fell in love with.

We were in Paris for a year, then it was back to One Victoria Street. I already knew what would happen as we locked the flat for the final time. Inevitable, unstoppable brimming.

LAURA FREEMAN, like Linda Radlett, hopes one day to become '*une femme sérieuse*'. If only she would read a bit less Madame de Pompadour and a bit more Proust.

A Leap into the Light

DEREK JOHNS

I first met Jan Morris in the offices of the publisher Random House in New York in the early 1980s. I was a junior editor there, and was invited to meet someone I considered to be one of the most intriguing writers I had read. This was nothing more than a handshake and an acknowledgement of our shared Britishness in New York. But I was immediately struck by Jan's warmth and affability, qualities that are key to her genius for talking to people and drawing stories from them. (For while Jan is less of an extrovert in person than in her writings, and indeed in some ways is quite reserved, she nonetheless possesses a remarkable ability, surely learned in the world of journalism, to nose out a story.)

Ten years later I had the privilege of becoming Jan's literary agent at A. P. Watt, taking over from somebody who had left the firm. I remained in this role until I retired from full-time agenting in 2013. We stayed in touch, however, and our meetings led to my writing a short book about her, *Ariel: A Literary Life of Jan Morris*.

Her own memoir, *Conundrum*, had first been published in 1974, just two years after the gender reassignment operation that turned James Morris into Jan, and which had created a sensation. Such operations had been conducted before, but not on anyone whose profile stood as high as James Morris's. Furthermore, he was in some ways a man's man, one of the leading journalists of his day, the author of scoops on the Everest expedition of 1953 and the Suez débâcle of 1956. That such a man should choose to become a woman seemed extraordinary. Thousands of letters poured in, as well as invitations to appear on television and radio in Britain and elsewhere. As Jan observes in her memoir, 'Half a lifetime of diligent craftsmanship had done far less for my reputation than a simple change of sex!'

Conundrum is the nearest thing Jan has written to an autobiography. But as she herself acknowledges, in a sense all her writing is auto-biographical. Her books represent con-versations between Jan Morris and the places she is writing about. Her approach is wholly subjective, and it is hardly an exaggeration to say that she has imposed her personality on the entire world. Yet *Conundrum* is indeed unique among her books. It is a wise, witty and profoundly moving account of an experience which is surely almost impossible to communi-cate to those who have not themselves gone through it.

James Morris on the 1953 Everest expedition

The book begins with the simple statement that Jan was 'three or four years old when I realized that I had been born into the wrong body, and should really be a girl'. As this conviction grew, James was 'not unhappy' but 'habitually puzzled'. He went to the Cathedral Choir School at Christ Church in Oxford, and then to Lancing College, having 'fumbling' homosexual experiences along the way. But his wish to be female was not about sex, rather about spirit. In the British Army, as James and his friend Otto rode in the back of a truck on a starlit night in the Suez Canal Zone, Otto turned to him and stammered 'G-g-god . . . I w-wish you were a woman.' This wish, James's own fervent wish, became increasingly hard to bear, and in the end he had to do something about it.

In recent years transgendering has become almost fashionable. There are stories about it in newspapers and magazines practically every day. Tom Hooper's adaptation of David Ebershoff's novel *The Danish Girl*, starring Eddie Redmayne, was a great success (Hooper crediting *Conundrum* as an important source of inspiration and information, by the way). It is perhaps difficult for us now to appreciate just how momentous a decision this was for James in the 1960s and early 1970s. The sheer bravery of the act is easy to underestimate. James was about to change his 'form and apparency – my status too, perhaps my place among my peers . . . my reputation, my manner of life, my prospects, my emotions, possibly my abilities'. What would the ultimate consequences be? He couldn't then know.

The first transgender operations were carried out in Germany in 1930. The word used then was 'transsexualism', not 'transgender', and it was only towards the end of the twentieth century that the word transgender came into common use. An early case was that of Lili Elbe, the 'Danish girl' of the book and film. By the 1960s such operations were if not commonplace then at least carried out routinely. For people in Britain the most famous instance was that of April Ashley. But people who were willing to adopt such an extreme remedy were nonetheless still considered freaks. Were their problems physiological or psychological? To this day there appears to be no firm consensus on this. In an introduction to the 2001 edition of *Conundrum* Jan wrote of research which suggested that a region of the hypothalamus, at the floor of the brain, was abnormally small in transsexuals. But there is no widely agreed hypothesis on the subject. Jan takes little interest nowadays in the subject of transgendering, however. Her feeling is that it was all a very long time ago and that she has said all she wants to say about it in her book.

The strength of feeling Jan Morris expresses about James's condition is often startling.

> My work was well-known on both sides of the Atlantic, and the opportunities I was offered were almost unbounded. But I wanted none of it. It was repugnant to me. I thought of public success itself, I suppose, as part of maleness, and I deliberately turned my back on it, as I set my face against manhood . . . I was cultivating impotence.

This feeling that James's body was not just wrong but hateful is one that caused him utter despair in his thirties. He even contemplated suicide. And yet there is a remarkable context to these feelings, since James Morris was at the time the loving husband of his wife Elizabeth and the equally loving father of four children. (There was a fifth child, who died at the age of two weeks; this is movingly described in *Conundrum*.)

James and Elizabeth met in London shortly after the end of the Second World War and were married in 1949. James told Elizabeth about his feelings at the outset, and Elizabeth accepted them. Not the least remarkable aspect of Jan Morris's life is that the marriage survived and transcended the problems posed by James's condition. Furthermore, the children, who were aged between around 9 and 17 during the time of the transition, have stoutly supported Jan throughout. For a time Jan and Elizabeth maintained separate households, Jan in Oxford and later Bath, and Elizabeth in North Wales, but the relationship never foundered. In 2008 they were formally reunited in a civil partnership ceremony. They live together in the converted stable block of the *plas*, the big house they owned for many years near the village of Llanystumdwy in Gwynedd.

Naturally one of the questions readers of *Conundrum* have asked is 'What about sex?' Jan is perhaps a little evasive about this, and understandably so. Her desire to be a woman was not about wanting to have sexual relations with men, though she does rather charmingly describe the pleasures of being flirted with. A marriage that produces four children must be to some extent sexually healthy. But it is to Jan's credit as a writer that the reader does not dwell on this for long. We accept that for her, sex was not so much a physical as a spiritual matter.

Jan Morris wrote *Conundrum* very soon after the operation, and by now, nearly fifty years after the event, it seems clear that it is describing a transitional emotional state. Jan writes:

The more I was treated as a woman, the more a woman I

became. I adapted willy-nilly. If I was assumed to be oddly incompetent at reversing cars, or opening bottles, oddly incompetent I found myself becoming . . . Men treated me more and more as a junior . . . and so, addressed every day of my life as an inferior, involuntarily, I accepted the condition. I discovered that even now, men prefer women to be less informed, less able, less talkative and certainly less self-centred than they are themselves: so I generally obliged them.

Many women readers have objected strongly to this characterization. It was as though, having been a chivalrous man, Jan now wanted to be a damsel in distress. Some critics stated flatly that while she might have undergone a physical transformation, she had no idea what it was actually like to be a woman. Jan claimed to have become more emotional. 'I cried very easily, and was ludicrously susceptible to sadness or flattery. Finding myself less interested in great affairs . . . I acquired a new concern for small ones. My scale of vision seemed to contract, and I looked less for the grand sweep than the telling detail.'

For anyone who knows the Jan Morris of today and has read fairly widely in James/Jan's oeuvre, these statements written in 1973 sound unconvincing. And Jan would appear now to accept this. I suspect there is no real difference between what Jan Morris in her later life has been as a person and a writer, and what James Morris would have been had he remained a man. As regards her competence, anyone who has had the experience of being a passenger in her car as she drives down the rutted road to her home will attest to her skills and enthusiasm.

In her writing, while some critics for a while claimed to detect a change in tone, I don't think there is any persuasive evidence for such a change. The sensibility, conditioned early by High Anglican Christianity and shaped by readings of the King James Bible and Shakespeare, remained a constant. *Conundrum* itself remains an essential book, one of the seminal books of the late twentieth century. Its importance may be considered alongside that of Simone de Beauvoir's *The Second Sex* and Germaine Greer's *The Female Eunuch*. It has been a beacon whose light has stretched far and wide. Jan Morris was a pioneer not in that she took the brave step she did, but in that she was able, with her superb literary gifts, to communicate her experience so powerfully to other people, many of whom shared the distress and confusion she herself had felt. *Conundrum* is a modern classic.

DEREK JOHNS has been a bookseller, editor, publisher and literary agent. He is a former trustee of English PEN, a member of the Advisory Committee of the Booker Foundation, and an Honorary Fellow of the Royal Society of Literature.

Jan Morris's *Conundrum* (200pp) is now available in a limited and numbered cloth-bound edition of 2,000 copies (subscriber price: UK & Eire £17, Overseas £19; non-subscriber price: UK & Eire £18.50, Overseas £20.50). All prices include post and packing. Copies may be ordered by post (53 Hoxton Square, London N1 6PB), by phone (020 7033 0258) or via our website www.foxedquarterly.com.

Commons People

ROWENA MACDONALD

When I first started working at the House of Commons, back in 2001, Philip Hensher was still discussed in dark tones by my colleagues. He was the only employee in living memory to have been sacked. Five years before, he had written *Kitchen Venom*, a novel set in the Clerks' Department where we worked, about John, a secretly gay, hunchbacked senior clerk who spends his workday afternoons sneaking off to see a beautiful Italian rent boy in Earls Court.

Hensher wasn't sacked for the novel, per se, although senior management weren't entirely happy about his depiction of clerks as workshy fops who have no respect for the MPs they advise and who 'treat Members to their faces with civility, and behind their backs as inferior undergraduates who have mistaken their ambitions'. The sackable offence came while Hensher was publicizing *Kitchen Venom*. He gave an interview to *Attitude* in which he expounded upon how many Members were gay, how ugly most of them were and which ones he found attractive. He revealed he had always rather liked Gordon Brown's 'shagged-out look'.

My colleagues were primarily upset by what they viewed as thinly veiled poison-pen portraits of certain individuals, and, according to Hensher, in an interview in the *Independent*, by small details such as

the clerks sitting round composing lists of the 20 stupidest MPs in the House. It was just too galling to have someone say that

Philip Hensher, *Kitchen Venom* (1996)
Flamingo · Pb · 336pp · £9.99 · ISBN 9780007152421

Commons life is full of people playing stupid games. But then the point of the book is the interplay between ordinary human beings and the jobs they occupy.

When I read the book, I could vaguely recognize some traits of some people (others had since retired), but it was hard to understand why my colleagues couldn't view the novel objectively and judge it on its literary merits.

Kitchen Venom is set in 1990, during the lead-up to Thatcher's forced resignation. Thatcher appears herself at intervals throughout the novel, reflecting grandly on her power and the loss of it and sometimes acting as an omniscient narrator of the main characters' stories. This lends the novel part of its off-kilter quality.

After a prelude in which the Prime Minister relates an anxiety dream about her loss of power, the novel starts with the funeral of John's unpopular wife. Hensher relishes the social awkwardness of the occasion, detailing the hypocritical conversations about the dead woman and the conventional platitudes that everyone, apart from John's drunken elder daughter Jane, feels obliged to spout.

Jane and her sister Francesca are 31 and 29 respectively. Neither works, both are single and both still live in the family home, somewhere in an unnamed but obviously upmarket area of London. Francesca, who has adopted this more exotic version of her real name, Frances, is a passive aggressive, affected pain in the neck. 'She moved through her life as if expecting to be looked at . . . Those who noticed her often felt that they were being instructed in Francesca's mood by her posture. Sometimes they went along with it . . . More often, they looked at her and were enraged.' Jane is permanently enraged by her sister.

Jane and Francesca are like two Edwardian spinsters lolling about in a drawing-room with not enough to do. Their upper-middle-class milieu and the unchanging nature of the House of Commons, in which many scenes are set, give the novel, if not quite an archaic quality, then a curious timelessness. Hensher seems to be channelling the spirit of Ivy Compton-Burnett; indeed, John's colleague Henry has read all her novels and at one point lends *Two Worlds and Their Ways* to Francesca.

Hensher's tone has a similar cold, drawling wit and urbane subversiveness – a funeral guest is like 'a dwarf in Velázquez, blackly festive'; at the funeral the guests eat asparagus – 'And when they pissed, the stink of asparagus would remind them of what they had eaten, and where they had been'; a murder scene is ruthlessly dispatched in one sudden line. He breaks conventional rules about dialogue serving plot and allows idle conversations to continue long enough for characters to be hoist by their own petards. His style also borrows from the 'smooth unfeeling poetry' of the Journal of the House, in which the proceedings of the House of Commons have been recorded in a quasi-biblical, quasi-legalistic tone since the sixteenth century.

John is the Clerk of the Journals and, as John Walsh noted in the *Independent*, Hensher views the Journal as 'a large and potent metaphor of human behaviour':

They kept the minutes of the House, which was called the Journal of the House. Everything needs its minutes to be kept. Everything needs to be reduced from what occurs to what it means. We are human, and we cannot write down what happened, not everything that happened. We can only write down the significance of the events, in the end; we can only write down, and record, the decisions that are come to.

My favourite parts of *Kitchen Venom* are the descriptions of the House of Commons itself, which convey its cloistered, claustrophobic atmosphere.

The corridors; the hundreds of stairs; the thousands of windowed rooms looking out on windowed curtained courts and
spires and a scrap of sky. Whenever [he] walked, lost, through
the corridors of the Palace, they were so dimly lit; so silent,
private and, in their green warm light, so underwater, that into
his mind often came the thought 'The secret Ministry'. In this
public place, into which the public never came, upon which so
many thoughts were daily bent, he walked, removed from the
world of men, unsuspected by any, unheard, unwatched in this
secret place, performing his secret ministry. He had no hidden
purpose, but he felt like an anarchist when he walked the
streets, hiding the round black bomb of his job.

In *The Threat Level Remains Severe*, my own novel about the
House, I explore its archaic absurdities and its beguiling secretiveness,
the sense of being in an enclosed world with its own peculiar rules,
cut off from supposed real life. It's this secretive quality and the
secretiveness of the clerks themselves, the impassive role they are
supposed to play, contrasted with their hidden hatreds and desires,
that form the backbone of *Kitchen Venom*. You sense Hensher is
speaking through Jane when, at her mother's funeral, she says to
Henry that his job is 'like a mask or a coffin' and observes, 'Look at
John. You can see he's sad but it's all terribly public . . . All that self-
control. The way he's taking it, it's so correct and public. He never
stops. None of you do.'

The novel is character- rather than plot-driven; it's an unnerving,
modulated chamber piece, in which the most dramatic events are not
described. To explain the story fully would risk spoilers, so I'll give a
coy summary.

After the funeral, John continues to visit Giacomo, his handsome
rent boy. He loves the secrecy of these illicit assignations, beyond
wanting to keep up respectable appearances. 'He relished secrecy, and
he created it around him. Perhaps it was why he decided to do the

job that he did. He was secretive about it even when there was no need.' His new junior colleague, Louis, is also gay but 'out'. While walking through Trafalgar Square together one day after work, they bump into Giacomo. Although John pretends Giacomo is one of his daughter's friends, Louis understands immediately the true nature of their relationship. His understanding and what he does with this knowledge have terrible consequences.

In the seventeen years I have worked in the House of Commons, it has become less stuffy and cut off from the outside world. The Clerks' Department has gone through several name changes and is now the cosily inclusive Chamber and Committees Team. My own job title has changed from 'secretary' to the more gender-neutral 'committee assistant'. The old brand of clerks, who were knowledgeable about opera and could name all the novels of Trollope, as they do in *Kitchen Venom*, are now nearing retirement and the new clerks are eager young people with a terrifying work ethic, who did not all go to Oxbridge and are not all men. We now have a normal amount of annual leave, rather than the languorous recesses Hensher's characters enjoy. Some of these changes are for the better but, overall, the place has become blander. In my own novel, the House is on the cusp of change, but its new, more corporate rules still force people to dissemble, and those who don't play by these rules are deemed failures.

The entire time I was writing, I worried about getting sacked if my novel were published. In the end, I happened to meet Hensher at a book launch. His advice was 'Publish and be damned . . . after all it worked out quite well for me in the end.' And so I did. So far, I have not been sacked. But then again, I haven't yet revealed to any magazines which MPs I fancy.

ROWENA MACDONALD's first collection of short stories, *Smoked Meat*, was shortlisted for the 2012 Edge Hill Prize. Her first novel, *The Threat Level Remains Severe*, was shortlisted for the *Guardian*'s Not the Booker Prize in 2017. She still works at the House of Commons.

A Perfect Electrometer

ROGER HUDSON

My Cambridge tutor was bubbling over with pleasure one morning in 1962 after reading Dorothy Wordsworth's journal, the one she kept between 1800 and 1803 when living with her poet brother William at Dove Cottage in the Lake District. What he had been particularly taken with was something she wrote on 14 May 1802 when the two had been walking in the woods alongside Grasmere: 'William teased himself with seeking an epithet for the Cuckow.' I never forgot this slightly comical picture of the creative process, but it was almost thirty years before I came to read her journal myself when doing a book on Coleridge among the lakes and mountains.

I suspect my tutor had bought a copy of the Pelican paperback called *Home at Grasmere* which appeared in 1960, compiled by Colette Clark. She had had the clever idea of interleaving extracts from the journal with the Wordsworth poems most closely linked to them. In 1969 her father Kenneth Clark, in the eleventh chapter of *Civilisation*, 'The Worship of Nature', was to call Dorothy 'this shy, unassuming woman . . . the saint and prophetess' of the new religion of the Romantics. Just after he had met her for the first time, in June 1797, Coleridge wrote of her manners – 'simple, ardent, impressive'

There are several editions of Dorothy Wordsworth's journals available. See also Colette Clark (ed.), *Home at Grasmere: Extracts from the Journal of Dorothy Wordsworth and from the Poems of William Wordsworth* (1960) · Penguin · Pb · 304pp · £12.99 · ISBN 9780140431360. Robert Gittings's biography of Dorothy, which he wrote with his wife Jo Manton and which was published in 1985, is now out of print but we can obtain second-hand copies.

– of 'her most innocent soul' – of 'her eye watchful in minutest observation of nature' – of her taste, 'a perfect electrometer'. He had seen at once the qualities that were soon to make her such a vital auxiliary in his and Wordsworth's creative, collaborative uprush among the Quantock Hills in Somerset that led to the *Lyrical Ballads*, and then during the attempt to rekindle those hotbed days starting a year or more later and hundreds of miles to the north, among the Lakes. But what has been abundantly clear since her Grasmere journal was first published in 1897 is that it is itself priceless and incomparable, called by Robert Gittings, the Keats and Hardy expert and her biographer, 'the prime example in our literature of a purely unconscious masterpiece'.

Some stand out among those who have written about nature: Coleridge himself in his notebooks, Francis Kilvert, Gerard Manley Hopkins, Richard Jefferies and, closer to our day, perhaps John Stewart Collis and Robert Macfarlane. For many Dorothy Wordsworth remains first among equals in this band. The effects of light and shade, mist and cloud, sunlight, moonshine and starlight; water falling as rain, as a lake's surface, as a rushing stream, or when throwing itself over a waterfall; the birds and beasts, including her neighbours' cows of which she was rather frightened, and the sheep; the flowers, moss, grass and trees, particularly the oaks and birches – these were what caught her eye, alone or in combination, as when 'the moon shone like herrings in the water', or when they formed into a view.

Like Kilvert she was an avid recorder of noises – 'the small birds are singing, lambs bleating, cuckow calling, the thrush sings by fits. Thomas Ashburner's axe is going quietly (without passion) in the orchard. Hens are cackling, flies humming, the women talking together at their doors.' Like nearly all before about 1820, she had as background the luxury of silence and, at night, darkness. In those days everybody lived much closer to the weather, but where she and the Romantics in general – Turner in particular – were different was in their urge to get it down on canvas or paper, to transform a mere topic of conversation into an accessory or outright subject of art.

What was it in the Wordsworth family background that threw up the pairing of the 'exquisite sister' and her brother? The very lack of family seems to be the answer. Their mother had died in 1778, when Dorothy was 7; she never saw her father from that point until his death in 1783. She went first to live with an exemplary cousin in Halifax then, aged 15, to her mother's dour parents in Penrith, before escaping with an uncle and his wife to their Norfolk rectory in 1788, where she immersed herself in parish visiting, running the Sunday school and, in her words, acting as 'head nurse, housekeeper and tutoress' of her young cousins. Only occasionally did she see her four brothers; William went to Cambridge then, swept up in the revolutionary fervour, was in France in 1791–2, leaving just before the birth of his daughter by his French lover, Annette Vallon, and the outbreak of war.

Dorothy was totally accepting of this, but her uncle would not have William in Norfolk, so in 1794 she left, made a visit to the Lakes with him and began a tour round her relations while he went off to try and find a way out of his troubles. They only met up again in mid-1795, when William had been left a bit of money and then had the offer of a house, rent-free, south of Chard in Dorset. Suddenly the opportunity of a home of their own, of family life was there. The healing process could commence, they could start to open out and give nature full attention, while Dorothy's simplicity and clarity of vision could begin to help lead William away from the tired and confining 'poetic' diction of the day. He was later to say, 'She gave me eyes, she gave me ears.'

Then in June 1797 Coleridge descended on their new domesticity and like some pied piper led them off to Nether Stowey in north Somerset where he and his family had set up house. Firmly under his spell, they moved to Alfoxden nearby until the end

of June 1798 and there from January to April she kept her first surviving journal. On 2 February they went for a walk with Coleridge after dinner. 'A very clear afternoon. We lay sidelong upon the turf, and gazed upon the landscape until it melted into more than natural loveliness. The sea very uniform, of a pale greyish blue, only one distant bay, bright blue as a sky; had there been a vessel sailing up it, a perfect image of delight.' On 22 March she spent the morning starching and hanging out linen, then the next day Coleridge came to dine, bringing with him his completed *Ancient Mariner.*

The mix of hypersensitive, supercharged observation with mundane domestic detail is present from the start, and one is grateful for it: the one without the other would be intolerable. Dorothy was constantly occupied: cooking, baking, making, mending and altering clothes, starching, ironing, working in the garden, dealing with its seasonal surpluses of gooseberries, peas or beans, or the fish caught by the menfolk in the lake. Then there was William's poetry to be copied out, correspondence with friends and relations to be kept up, books to be read, German studied, visitors entertained and accommodated, while William's and her own very regular ailments had to be dealt with and endured, as had the frequently foul weather. Her reward for her labours was to be able to walk, in the daytime and often at night, in the incomparable landscape which she then managed by magic to preserve for us in her journal, to which William often turned for inspiration or as an aide-memoire.

[11 October 1800] After dinner we walked up Greenhead Gill in search of a sheepfold . . . The colours of the mountains soft and rich, with orange fern [bracken], the cattle pasturing upon the hill-tops, kites sailing in the sky above our heads, sheep bleating and in lines and chains and patterns scattered over the mountains. They come down and feed on the little green islands in the beds of the torrents and so may be swept away . . . Look down the brook and see the drops rise upwards and sparkle in the air. [See William's poem 'Michael'.]

The most famous example is Dorothy's description on 15 April 1802 of a belt of daffodils alongside Ullswater, which 'tossed and reeled and danced and . . . looked so gay, ever dancing, ever changing'. William was not to write 'I wandered lonely as a cloud' until 1804. On the other hand, a month earlier, on 13 March, he had been trying to write a poem about their encounter with a tall beggar woman and her sons in June 1800. When Dorothy read her journal entry about it to him, 'an unlucky thing it was for he could not escape from those very words, and so he could not write the poem'. Between those two dates comes that 'divine morning', and wonderful juxtaposition, on 27 March, when 'At breakfast Wm wrote part of an ode. Mr Olliff sent the dung and Wm went to work in the garden. We sate all day in the orchard.' This was not just any old ode, but rather the start of 'Intimations of Immortality' – divine indeed.

The spring of 1802 was a period of inspiration to match the one in 1797–8 in the Quantocks, but this time only for William. Coleridge had come with his family to live in Keswick, about twelves miles north of Grasmere, in July 1800, hoping to revive the Somerset experience. However, he was much troubled, out of love with his wife whom Dorothy saw was quite unsuited to him, and at the same time hopelessly smitten with Sara Hutchinson. He was increasingly resorting to laudanum and the brandy bottle and in October 1800 Wordsworth refused to include his poem 'Christabel', which he had recently completed, in the second edition of the *Lyrical Ballads*. This was a blow which his biographer Richard Holmes thinks effectively killed his ability to compose poetry as such, so instead he wrote those remarkable prose descriptions to be found in his notebooks.

The culmination of the Grasmere journal is not about the Lakes at all, but covers the period from July 1802, when William and Dorothy were able to visit his daughter and her mother in Calais during the brief Peace of Amiens, until they returned to Yorkshire where William married his long-time sweetheart Mary Hutchinson in October. She was the elder sister of the Sara with whom Coleridge was in love, and an old and close friend of Dorothy. In *Civilisation* Kenneth Clark made play with what he saw as a parallel: 'Both Byron and Wordsworth fell deeply in love with their sisters. The inevitable prohibition was a disaster for both of them.' He claimed Wordsworth suffered most because at least Byron wrote *Don Juan,* 'whereas Wordsworth, after the heart-breaking renunciation of Dorothy, gradually lost inspiration'.

This last is undeniable. Graham Hough, Cambridge Professor of English, recalled how he 'once knew a man in a prison camp who divided his copy of Wordsworth's poems into two halves, retained the first, and swapped the second for the bottom half of a pair of pyjamas. He rightly judged that the intellectual loss was very slight.' But while the relationship between Byron and his half-sister Augusta Leigh was what we might call full-on, the love between the Wordsworths was something else. She may have written, one day when he was away, 'O the Darling! Here is one of his bitten apples! I can hardly find it in my heart to throw it in the fire,' and on another how they sat at the window – 'I on a chair and William with his hand on my shoulder. We were in deep Silence and Love, a blessed hour.' But these were expressions of a mutual devotion without a sexual element, which saw Dorothy accompanying the newlyweds in the post-chaise back to Grasmere and there forming a triangular household with them. She was soon deeply absorbed, housekeeping as before, helping Mary with her pregnancies and looking after her and William's children. In January 1803 she had written what turned out to be her last journal entry at Dove Cottage, and it was not because of any heartbreak, but because she was too busy.

ROGER HUDSON last visited Dove Cottage in 2016 and left it moved, but glad not to have had to live there. The wood engravings in this article are by Reynolds Stone.

In the Eye of the Storm

POSY FALLOWFIELD

Anyone who has read – or started to read – *The Human Predicament* by Richard Hughes probably shares my frustration that it remained unfinished on his death in 1976. Hughes had planned a trilogy, tracing the origins of the Second World War through a clever amalgam of fact and fiction. Hitler's rise to power, including his early failures, is faithfully documented, and interwoven with this impressively researched truth is the fictitious story of a family with both German and English branches. The first in the trilogy, *The Fox in the Attic*, was published in 1961 to resounding acclaim – an Italian critic declared, 'England has found her Tolstoy' – and the second, *The Wooden Shepherdess*, followed in 1973. Sadly, Hughes only completed twelve chapters of the third and final volume and twentieth-century literature is the poorer for it.

Consolingly, I recently discovered Hughes's *In Hazard*, published in 1938. (*A High Wind in Jamaica*, his best-known novel, appeared even earlier, in 1929.) The dust jacket didn't immediately appeal, promising 'high suspense on the high seas . . . [an] unremitting struggle for survival . . . [an] eerie fascination with the hurricane . . . [a] wrenching tale of humanity at its limits'. To a non-sailor it sounded both exhausting and forbiddingly nautical. However, recalling how much I'd enjoyed his other books I decided to try it (thinking, shamefully, that at 160 pages it wouldn't be too arduous).

I loved it. *In Hazard* is an extraordinary read. It resembles *The*

Richard Hughes, *In Hazard* (1938), is available as a print-on-demand edition. We can also obtain second-hand copies.

Human Predicament in mixing fiction with fact, but here the 'fact' is not a devastating political movement which took years to grow, but a devastating meteorological event which took place within a week. In November 1932 the steamship *Phemius* was sucked into a Caribbean hurricane and tested to the limits, yet somehow she and all her crew survived. The owner of the shipping line to which *Phemius* belonged approached Hughes and suggested he record the dramatic story. Hughes agreed to describe the storm and its effects on the ship as accurately as he could, with the proviso that he would invent a fictitious captain and crew. He researched the project rigorously, interviewed the crew, sailed with the *Phemius*'s captain and became familiar with every inch of a 'single-screw turbine steamer of a little over 9,000 tons'.

From the outset Hughes takes the reader by the hand, explaining with sparkling clarity how a steamship – his is the *Archimedes* – works. He escorts us both above and below decks, detailing everything in a conversational, matter-of-fact way. Then, having guided us around the *Archimedes*' engine-room and fire-room, he shows us, almost reverently, the propeller-shaft – 'the quiet, simple thing that all this is about'.

> Think of a tree. The roots of a tree spread in a most complicated manner through the ground, extracting all kind of necessary things. This nourishment passes, unified, up the plain column of its trunk, and bursts out in the air into a countless multitude of leaves. So all the varying forces, the stresses and resistances, proceeding from that welter of machinery, are unified into the simple rotation of this horizontal column: are conducted calmly along its length into the sea: and there burgeon suddenly into the white and glass-green foliage of the swirls, the tumbling currents, the enormously powerful jostling of crowded water which is a ship's wake.

And now we realize we are in the hands of a novelist – or perhaps ('glass-green foliage' is inspired) a poet. Yes, he is an experienced sailor who knows this steamship inside out, but he is imaginative too and understands precisely how to impart his knowledge. We are shown how a propeller works; and I defy anyone to describe better a ship's wake.

Hughes also moves comfortably between fact and invention. The ship's officers, being fictitious, allow him to examine different facets of human nature. He conjures some of the men's backgrounds, engaging our sympathies for their coming ordeal.

Subtly, he instils tension from the start. Anyone picking up the book will know what they are in for – my copy has a queasy cover photograph of, simply, a heaving sea beneath a filthy orange sky – and his reassurance at the outset that the *Archimedes* is a 'fine ship' is small comfort. The more he reassures, the more anxious we become. Somehow it's no help to hear about the strength of the funnel guys. ('When these guys were properly set up, that funnel was as safe as the Bank of England.') Later, he says the wheel on the bridge effortlessly operates the steering-gear, 'and should the wheel . . . for any reason be out of action, there is a second, emergency wheel in the stern. But should the steam steering-engine itself fail, why, then you would be in a hole.' He exudes breezy confidence. But that 'you' has press-ganged us, embroiled us in whatever is to come. If there is to be a 'hole' then we will be in it.

He declares that modern meteorology protects shipping. 'The days of Conrad's *Typhoon* are passed . . . when hurricanes pounced on shipping as unexpectedly as a cat on mice.' He is playing with us, of course; every confident assertion only unnerves us further. Then we learn that the storm 'was not at all where it was thought by the pundits to be' and somehow the *Archimedes* has been caught. A junior officer, whose first hurricane this is, hopes for drama, 'something spectacular . . . for letters home'. But Hughes instead emphasizes the unremarkable:

No . . . nor was it a Viking figure that stood at the wheel: it was a little old Chinese quartermaster, with a face like a wrinkled yellow apple, standing on a little old mat.

That inspired novelistic touch of the 'little old Chinese quartermaster' on his 'little old mat' achieves two things superbly. First it underlines the ship's fragility as the storm gathers power. And second it makes us believe utterly in the truth of the story. Why else mention a 'little old mat' if it were not there, before our eyes?

Hughes's descriptive powers are unleashed with the storm. 'The ship might just as well have been standing up on its stern when you tried to go forward: and coming aft was like falling downstairs.' The imagery is commonplace, almost prosaic. He adds: 'And over the side one saw, not the familiar sea, but rather whole countrysides of water.'

It gets steadily worse. Hatches are whipped off and somehow, in a terrifying wind, repaired. Men find courage to do extraordinary things. The Chinaman is indeed blown off the bridge on his 'inadequate toboggan: then fetched up against the rails . . . with such a terrific impact as to bend them' but he is dragged back. The wheel stops steering, the double-skinned funnel is torn clean away, steam escapes – eventually everything fails. A ship dependent on steam has no other resources: 'she was dead, as a log is dead, rolling in the sea; she was not a ship any more'.

He describes heroism, raw fear, human frailty. A few men waver, one cracks altogether, but most find astonishing reserves of bravery and endurance. The Captain, fortunately, has 'enough courage to serve out round the ship in ladles'.

Eventually, in the eye of the storm, the men can at last see clearly, but the nightmare only intensifies:

> Now you could see the horizon tilted sideways, the whole ocean tipped up at a steep slope as if about to pour over the edge of the world: so steep that it seemed to tower over the lee bulwarks. It was full of sharks, too, which looked at you on your own level . . .

In the lull, birds alight on the ship. 'Some herons even tried to settle on the lee bulwarks, that were mostly awash; and were picked like fruit by the sharks.' The decks are now oily and birds stick 'like flies on a flypaper. The officers kept stepping on live birds – they could not help it . . . I must tell you what things were like . . . you would feel the delicate skeleton scrunch under your feet; the gummed feathers hardly even fluttered.' Then, with the storm renewing, the battle begins again. For six days, despite exhaustion and hunger, the crew struggle to handle the failing ship in ferocious weather.

Finally, however, the *Archimedes* is rescued and the Captain rejoices, 'We haven't lost a man!' Then Hughes – ever the novelist – delivers one heartbreaking death almost as an afterthought.

In a fascinating Afterword, he suggested – with hindsight – that he'd been eager to write this book because, subconsciously, the struggle of the steamship and her crew had symbolized the coming war. 'In our bones we had foreseen from the very beginning this hurricane of preternatural power which no manoeuvring could dodge.' It evidently struck a chord with readers, because by 1945 sales of *In Hazard* had outstripped those of *A High Wind in Jamaica*; but whether you read it as symbol or documentary, as fiction or fact, I guarantee you will not forget it.

POSY FALLOWFIELD lives in Devon where she enjoys gardening and walking, activities which take place on terra firma. Her article was a runner-up in our 2018 Writers' Competition.

Springtime Reflections

CHRIS SAUNDERS

Edward Thomas's *In Pursuit of Spring* has always felt like a book that's in pursuit of me. Published in April 1914, it traces the author's cycle ride from London to the Quantocks one Easter weekend in search of the perfect English springtime. In doing so, he visits a number of the places of my life, from south London where I used to live, to Salisbury Plain where my father grew up and where Thomas sees 'Saunderses' buried in a graveyard, to such obscure places as the Lion and Fiddle pub in Hilperton in Wiltshire, where I once spent the night for a friend's wedding. It is, to say the least, unnerving to find oneself preceded everywhere.

Thomas sometimes trades in this kind of spookiness, though, and usually when you least expect it. His short stories and essays are full of myths and uncanny experiences. As a writer he is now best known for his nature poetry, and *In Pursuit of Spring* certainly brims with his characteristically minute observations of his surroundings, such as this oak wood near Box Hill: 'Sometimes the grey trunks were washed faintly with light, the accumulated branch-work proved itself purplish, and here and there the snick of a lost bough was bright.'

You can almost smell the sylvan air, and this is one of Thomas's attractions. Born in the suburbs, his love of nature drove his devout wish to escape the noise and chaos of London. Like him, I have moved to the sticks and I feel he is speaking for me when he writes:

Edward Thomas, *In Pursuit of Spring* (1914)
Little Toller • Pb • 228pp • £12 • ISBN 9781908213433

Many days in London have no weather. We are aware only that it is hot or cold, dry or wet; that we are in or out of doors; that we are at ease or not.

But Thomas's writing is more than pastoral escapism. He often turns his retreat to the country into an assessment of himself and this is where *In Pursuit of Spring* becomes spooky, funny and also strangely wise.

I am not the only person who repeatedly crosses Thomas's path. The other major character apart from the author himself is the Other Man. He is a peculiar, mercurial figure who is first seen buying a chaffinch in order to set it free. This ludicrous wool-gatherer, a fellow wandering cyclist, is next seen sketching a weathervane in Morden while being jeered at by labourers and then, at greater length, in a pub in Salisbury.

This isn't the only time in Thomas's writing that he conjures up a doppelgänger. His poem 'The Other' concerns a similar adventure, with the poet going from pub to pub in search of a mysterious version of himself who is, irritatingly, funnier and more popular than he is. *In Pursuit of Spring*, though, really runs with the whole concept. One wonders what his publishers thought when he submitted the manuscript – this was supposed to be a bucolic guide to the Quantocks, but they had on their hands something richer and stranger. The scene between the two men in the Salisbury pub is enthralling but totally unrelated to the central theme of the book. They discuss clay pipes, at extraordinary and fascinating length. First, the Other Man talks of the pipe industry; then Thomas talks of his own favourite pipes. The two men seem to have bonded, until we find that the Other Man has suddenly become bored by the whole subject:

> The Other Man cared nothing for the matter. He awoke from the stupor to which he had been reduced by listening, and asked –

'Did you see that weathervane at Albury in the shape of a pheasant?

Weathervanes are the Other Man's true obsession. Just as Thomas bored him with his clay pipes, so he exasperates with his chain of observations on weathervanes: 'And not long after this, I was asleep,' Thomas says. This is a comic and very English vignette of the difficulties of conversation between new acquaintances – especially, no doubt, if you are a middle-class gentleman in Edwardian England, constrained by manners and upbringing as well as by your rather niche interests.

The real importance of this section only becomes clear later. During their last extended conversation, it emerges that the Other Man is actually a reflection of the author himself. We find that the Other Man has been commissioned to write countryside books for £50 apiece, which is the trade that Thomas followed in the years leading up to the Great War. The narrator's response is that of the non-writer: 'That is a lot of money for such a book! . . . And you are lucky to get money for doing what you like.' With a magical sleight of hand, Thomas transforms himself into a different character. He is no longer a writer (despite his name being on the cover) but a general member of the public happening to meet an author. That author is very much like Edward Thomas, a man with constant health worries, a man who writes because he has a family to support and feels he is nothing but a hack:

He rambled on and on about himself, his past, his writing, his digestion; his main point being that he did not like writing . . . He abused notebooks violently. He said that they blinded him to nearly everything that would not go into the form of notes; or, at any rate, he could not afterwards reproduce the great effects of Nature . . .

This impromptu interview culminates in the Other Man sitting on a sheep trough gloomily eating monkey nuts while Thomas enjoys the landscape of Cley Hill. Thomas obviously finds his own self-pity rather amusing. Is it any wonder that he comically bored himself to sleep in the pub in Salisbury?

This Olympian level of self-deprecation says something important to me, though. Thomas is, humorously and whimsically, admitting that he takes himself too seriously. He is indeed lucky to get money for doing what he likes. Thomas had fought tooth-and-nail with his father to allow him to become a writer rather than a civil servant. He was fortunate enough to have his first book published very young so that he could strike out on his own. His main love in life was wandering the paths and lanes of England, and the prose works that were commissioned from him – lovely books such as *The South Country* and *The Heart of England* – not only allowed him to pursue that love but paid him well enough to support a wife and three children.

In Pursuit of Spring sees Thomas recognizing his own ingratitude, and poking fun at himself for it. The Other Man is finally reduced to an absurd, skittish figure, who is last glimpsed riding off from Kilve church in Somerset having followed up an obscure Wordsworthian reference in a rather antic fashion: 'There *is* no weather-cock,' said the Other Man, laughing a little more freely and disappearing for the last time.

He is comic, a little unsettling, rather lovable and apparently irrelevant to the main point of the book, which is Thomas's exploration of a glorious English springtime. Thomas is making it clear that the book's the thing. Writers should leave their bruised egos out of it – they only get in the way of the story.

Without doubt Thomas's good-natured chiding can be extended to all those occasionally complaining writers and arty types who are paid (perhaps not as much as they would like) for following their passions rather than slaving in offices and banks and factories and mines. I include myself in that number. As an antiquarian bookdealer I am taken all over the country by books and literature, to hundreds of delightful places where I meet warm and fascinating people and see the most wonderful treasures, yet I complain about the travelling and railway timetables. *In Pursuit of Spring* acts upon me rather like Robert Burns's famous maxim: 'O wad some Power the giftie gie us/ To see oursels as ithers see us!' At the end of the book, the Other Man miles behind him, Thomas finds himself on the road to Bridgend and declares:

> I had found Winter's grave; I had found Spring, and I was confident that I could ride home again and find Spring all along the road. Perhaps I should hear the cuckoo by the time I was again at the Avon, and see cowslips tall on ditchsides and short on chalk slopes, bluebells in all hazel copses, orchises everywhere in the lengthening grass . . .

Spring is everywhere, and it is glorious and full of hope, and we are living a good life. It is funny that it takes someone as doubting as Thomas to lift up the mirror and force me to make a proper appraisal: I have to admit, I do actually enjoy myself.

CHRIS SAUNDERS has been an antiquarian bookseller at Henry Sotheran Ltd since 2004. He also writes and runs his own blog, SpeaksVolumes. He now lives in East Sussex but has found that, unfortunately, the rural life consists of commuting every day to London.

An Unusual Lexicographer

ANN KENNEDY SMITH

In the early 1980s, my summer job was helping out at the local newsagent's in my home town, a small seaside resort in Northern Ireland. Apart from dusty tourist guides and *Old Moore's Almanack*, there weren't many books for sale. Tidying the shelves one day, however, I came across a slim volume with an important-sounding title. Something told me that *The Spoken Word: A BBC Guide* was the book I had been wanting for a long time, without realizing it. I handed over £2 of my hard-earned wages, and took it with me when I went back to university that autumn.

Ever since then, books about words have piled up on my desk, including *Fowler's Modern English Usage*, a *Roget's Thesaurus* and the 1987 'Compact Edition' (still huge) of the *Oxford English Dictionary* which came with its own magnifying-glass. But over the years Robert Burchfield's little book – you might even call it a booklet – is the one that I have turned to most often. It helped me to learn how to write.

The Spoken Word, published in 1981, was produced in response to a wave of complaints to the British Broadcasting Corporation about falling standards in spoken English. A new era of broadcasting had begun in the 1970s, as the BBC changed from being the Reithian home of 'received pronunciation' to something broader, permitting more regional accents and informal language. Many people felt that the move towards linguistic diversity had gone too far, resulting in

---

Robert Burchfield, *The Spoken Word. A BBC Guide* (1981), is out of print but we can obtain second-hand copies.

what the critic Anne Karpf so eloquently described in 1980 as 'English as she is murdered on radio'.

The BBC felt that its broadcasters needed help in deciding what was acceptable and what was not, and commissioned a brief, no-nonsense guide from Dr Robert Burchfield. There was probably no one who knew the English language better, or how it had changed in recent times. Burchfield was the editor of the supplement to the *Oxford English Dictionary*, the great twelve-volume dictionary that had been published between 1879 and 1933. When he first took charge in 1957, Oxford University Press estimated that the work would produce a single volume within seven years. Instead the *Supplement* comprised 60,000 new entries, took up four large volumes and was not completed until 1986.

Robert Burchfield was, on the face of it, an unlikely lexicographer. Born in Waganui, New Zealand, in 1923, he later claimed that his parents had just one book in the house, a socialist tract. In 1944, while on wartime service in Italy, he stumbled across Frederick Bodmer's *The Loom of Language: A Guide to Foreign Languages for the Home Student*. It was a book that changed his life, sparking off a fascination with words and their origins. After the war, he was awarded a Rhodes scholarship and moved to Oxford, where he was taught by C. S. Lewis and J. R. R. Tolkien. Burchfield might easily have opted for a quiet, scholarly life working on Old Norse poetry, but instead he accepted the challenge of bringing the *Oxford English Dictionary* into the twentieth century.

Updating the *OED* was a monumental task, requiring dogged patience and a team of dedicated workers, one of them the young Julian Barnes. The first two volumes of the *Supplement* (A–G and H–N) appeared in 1972 and 1976 respectively and, to his surprise and delight, Burchfield became something of a celebrity. He was a genial figure who featured on *Desert Island Discs* and regularly appeared on radio and television to give his views on current trends in spoken English. 'I can't understand what the young are saying any more,' the

former Prime Minister Edward Heath grumbled to him on the BBC's
Nationwide in the summer of 1979.

In *The Spoken Word*, Burchfield managed to offer soothing reassurance to the querulous while politely confirming that the English
language was in flux, just as it always had been. 'In what follows', he
says at the beginning of the book,

> it is assumed that the speaker uses received Standard English in
> its 1980s form. The form of speech recommended is that of a
> person born and brought up in one of the Home Counties,
> educated at one of the established southern universities, and
> not yet so set in his ways that all linguistic change is regarded
> as unacceptable.

Although I hadn't at that time set foot in England (and I was a
'she' not a 'he') it was clear that *The Spoken Word* was aimed at anyone
who was interested in speaking and writing more clearly. Rather than
strict rules of pronunciation, vocabulary and grammar, the book has
'preferences'. Burchfield is like a knowledgeable friend who keeps a
steady hand on the tiller, pointing out the occasional treacherous
current and rocky outcrop while reassuring us that the boat is sea-
worthy and safe. You feel you can trust him.

Much of his advice on pronunciation is still pertinent: 'be careful
not to garble words', 'avoid the use of reduced forms like "gunna,
kinda, sorta, wanna"'. Other recommendations are showing their
age, as you might expect. Who now places the stress on the first
syllable of 'despicable' and 'temporarily', or makes the final 't' in
'restaurant' silent? And, for that matter, does anyone now worry
about the correct pronunciation of 'contumely'? (Three syllables, not
four, if you're wondering.) Burchfield is sanguine about such changes,
pointing out that 'the pronunciations that are not recommended
may well prevail, as time goes on, within a period of about half a
century'.

In the things that matter, *The Spoken Word* has stood the test of time well. Burchfield recommends avoiding clichés ('at the end of the day') and using an unnecessarily long word when a short one will do ('severe, harsh, cruel are better than "Draconian"'). Be precise, he advises broadcasters: instead of 'industrial action' 'specify the type: strike, work to rule, overtime ban, etc'. Such echoes of long-ago battles can be heard in his advice on how to pronounce 'dispute' (noun and verb). Burchfield prefers the stress on the second syllable for both but notes that 'the influence of usage by northern trade union leaders is tending to bring the form with initial stress into prominence'. It is a reminder of how our spoken language is a reflection of our times, in this case the early 1980s stand-offs between the trade unions and Margaret Thatcher's newly elected Conservative government ('first 'n' fully pronounced *and never* 'guv-ment').

As a lexicographer, Burchfield was aware that the English language was becoming increasingly informal. 'Slang is the language of the future,' he told those who questioned its inclusion in the *OED*. Some uses of vocabulary were less negotiable than others, however. He notes that using *disinterested* to mean uncaring 'attracts more comment from listeners than any other word in this list with the possible exception of *hopefully*'. In the sense of 'it is to be hoped [that]' this dangerous word is deployed 'only by the brave or by young people unaware of public hostility to the use', he warns. And even the bravest or most informal speaker should be aware of grammatical gaffes such as false concord. 'Every one of those present were members of the union' (Correctly: '*Every one* of those present *was a member* of the union').

It is hard to disagree with this (did broadcasters really need reminding?), but one wonders how necessary it was in the 1980s to be able to carry through a sentence with 'one' as a subject. Just in case, Burchfield quotes Iris Murdoch to show how it should be done.

One's best hope is to get into one of those 'holes' where one's two neighbours are eagerly engaged elsewhere, so that one can concentrate upon one's plate.

Relevant or not, such quotations make *The Spoken Word* a continuing pleasure to read. Although the guide is ostensibly about the spoken language, Burchfield's examples show how writers like George Bernard Shaw make anything possible. 'If it doesn't matter *who* anybody marries, then it doesn't matter *who* I marry and it doesn't matter *who* you marry.' Language, in the right hands, can do anything it wants.

The duality of his approach can be seen in the section in which Burchfield sides with Fowler in making the case for the occasional split infinitive, and offers his own preference:

Avoid splitting infinitives wherever possible but do not suffer undue remorse if a split infinitive is unavoidable for the natural and unambiguous completion of a sentence already begun.

Then the schoolmaster gives way to the romantic, and he gives Iris Murdoch's words as a 'model example' of a perfectly deployed infinitive: 'I wanted simply to tell you of my love.'

Robert Burchfield's job as a lexicographer was to be dispassionate about language, but *The Spoken Word* reveals him to be a lover of words and literature. He quotes from writers as disparate as Fielding, Carlyle and Jowett, and Dryden rubs shoulders with Graham Greene and Martin Amis. His enjoyment in writing the book is plain to see, and it is infectious. He would have agreed with Virginia Woolf who said that words are, by their nature, impossible to pin down:

you can catch them and sort them and place them in alphabetical order in dictionaries. But words do not live in dictionaries; they live in the mind.

Her own spoken words – the only known recording of her voice – were captured by a radio broadcast in 1937, when the BBC still saw itself as a guardian of the language. In *The Spoken Word* Burchfield reminds us that words, like butterflies, should never be imprisoned. They will always escape in any case.

Ten years after I bought *The Spoken Word*, I replied to an advertisement requesting 'a harmless drudge' and soon afterwards joined a team of lexicographers at Cambridge University Press. The first edition of the *Cambridge International Dictionary of English*, aimed at students of English as a second language, appeared in 1995 and was, I am pleased to say, a modest success. Nowadays, most people tend to consult an online dictionary or thesaurus, and it's easy to find free advice on grammar and 'good English' via the Internet. But for some of us, there will always be room on our desks for books about words.

ANN KENNEDY SMITH is a writer and researcher in Cambridge. She is no longer a harmless drudge, but still loves words.

Just Staying

JONATHAN LAW

So where were you when you heard that Alistair MacLeod had died? You've no idea? I thought not. The passing of Canada's greatest writer in April 2014 made few shockwaves in Britain, where his work remains almost unknown. To his admirers, and I am enthusiastically one, this is both a scandal and a puzzle. For most of us, the books were a very personal discovery, and our feelings about them are commensurately possessive. Don't say it too loud, but it's absolutely true: this reticent, unfashionable, determinedly unprolific writer was one of the great masters of prose fiction in our time.

In forty years MacLeod produced just sixteen short stories, later collected in *Island* (2002), and one not very long novel, the extraordinary *No Great Mischief* (1999). Notoriously, he wrote at glacial speed, toiling over each sentence by hand until its shape and heft and tune were exactly so. You could read the life's work in a weekend, but you mustn't: the stories demand to be savoured slowly, the way they were written. A MacLeod sentence is a tactile thing, with the hard but polished feel of a pebble in the hand. Yet the prose is not 'writerly' in any tiresome way: 'I like to think that I am telling a story rather than writing it,' MacLeod once said, and his work retains a strong sense of the speaking or even singing voice – of folk tales or Gaelic balladry.

If the work is small in bulk, it is fiercely precise in its focus. Nearly

Alistair MacLeod, *No Great Mischief* (1999) · Vintage · Pb · 272pp · £8.99 · ISBN 9780099283928; *Island: Collected Stories* (2002) · Vintage · Pb · 448pp · £9.99 · ISBN 9780099422327.

all of it is set on Cape Breton, the large island at the tip of Nova
Scotia where MacLeod grew up and to which he returned every summer. Like most Cape Bretoners, he was descended from Highland
Scots who arrived during the Clearances, bringing a Gaelic-speaking
culture that continues today. Traditionally, the islanders worked as
miners, loggers, small farmers and inshore fishermen, and MacLeod
tried all four occupations before lighting on a career in academia. His
characters tend to be torn between leaving in search of a wider life
and staying out of a sense of loyalty and belonging. Those who
remain feel trapped or abandoned, while the leavers are racked with
a sense of exile and guilt.

A small stage, then, but some large, pertinent themes: the rival
claims of tradition and modernity, of the tribe and the individual, of
nativism and assimilation. These are probably the themes of your
family history, as they are (in part) of mine. They also seem to be at
the hub of our present discontents.

MacLeod's first published story, 'The Boat', encapsulates all this
with brutal clarity. The narrator – an unhappy academic – recalls his
early life on Cape Breton, in a small fishing community where his
world was defined by his father, an autodidact with a yearning for
another life, and his mother, a figure of almost archaic rootedness.

My mother was of the sea, as were all her people, and her horizons were the very literal ones she scanned with her dark and fearless eyes.

While the father's room is a chaos of magazines and books, the house is otherwise ruled by a woman who boasts of not having read a thing since school. As time goes on, the daughters of the family grow restless, marry 'out' and move away. Although the narrator also longs to go, he is held back by pity for his father, whom he sees visibly ageing:

And there came into my heart a very great love for my father and I thought it was very much braver to spend a life doing what you do not want rather than selfishly following your own dreams . . . And I knew then that I could never leave him alone to suffer the iron-tipped harpoons which my mother would forever hurl into his soul . . . I told him one night very resolutely and very powerfully that I would remain with him as long as he lived and we would fish the sea together.

So father and son fish through the summer heat and the autumn mists and into the first snowy blasts – until one day 'I turned and he was not there and I knew even in that instant that he would never be again.' The old man's body is found a week later, 'And the fish had eaten his testicles and the gulls had pecked out his eyes.'

As the story ends we hear how the narrator has made a career in the States, while his mother stays at home, increasingly bitter that her only son will not return to fish the family's ancestral grounds. Despite himself, the narrator cannot escape a feeling that she is right: 'it is not an easy thing to know that your mother looks upon the sea with love and on you with bitterness because the one has been so constant and the other so untrue'.

Rather like Henry James, MacLeod plays infinitely subtle variations on a small number of themes and situations. In 'The Return', for example, a Montreal lawyer returns to Cape Breton, bringing his wife and 10-year-old son to meet his parents for the first time. 'You have been a long time coming home,' remarks the grandfather, still working the mines at the age of 76. There is awkward social comedy, but the thing no one forgets is the grandmother's great speech of reproach to her son, in which she speaks for the 'stayers' everywhere:

> Because in the end that is all there is – just staying. I have lost three children at birth but I've raised eight sons. I have one a lawyer and one a doctor who committed suicide, one who died in coal beneath the sea and one who is a drunkard and four who still work the coal like their father and those four are all I have that stand by me . . .

The son makes the obvious, common-sense objections – but these sound flimsy after the grand biblical cadences. MacLeod may avoid taking sides in these culture wars, but his nativists certainly get the best tunes.

The backward-looking, in-turned side of Cape Breton life is not glossed over. In 'The Road to Rankin's Point' the old tumbledown farm where Grandma lives alone is almost too neatly symbolic. The house stands at the end of a long, little-frequented road; it is sinking into the earth and its doors open inwards; there is no electricity, gas or telephone. Even the livestock come from 'fiercely inbred generations' who will eat hay only from these fields. Quite reasonably, Grandma's family are trying to nudge her into a home. But it is the stubborn, unreasonable old woman who gets, if not the last word, then the word that lasts:

> It does not matter that some things are difficult. No one has ever said that life is easy. Only that it is to be lived.

MacLeod once compared writing to playing an accordion: 'When I pull it out like this, it becomes a novel, and when I compress it . . . it becomes this intense short story.' *No Great Mischief* may lack the compression of the stories, but 'pulling it out' enabled MacLeod to extend the cast of characters and to deepen the sense of history, bringing the Highland past directly into the tale. This allows for the most concerted treatment of his great theme – the strength, and the danger, of tribal solidarity.

The novel's narrator is another of MacLeod's exiles – Alexander MacDonald, a wealthy orthodontist now living in Ontario but who is haunted by his youth on Cape Breton. His story unfolds in three broad time-phases: the present, where Alexander fixes the teeth of the rich while also trying to care for his older brother Calum, an alcoholic wreck; the remembered past, in which we gradually learn of the events that brought Calum to this pass; and the ancestral past, the tragic history that drove their great-great-great-grandfather across the ocean with his wife, children, dog and violin.

'Always look after your own blood' Alexander is taught as a boy, and it is a lesson that he is never permitted to forget. One winter night, his parents are drowned while crossing frozen waters on foot – a catastrophe that evokes one of the great set pieces in MacLeod's writing:

> The tide was going out when they vanished, leaving nothing but a lantern – perhaps tossed on to the ice by a sinking hand and miraculously landing upright and continuing to glow, or perhaps, set down after its arc, wildly but carefully by a hand which sought to reach another . . .

Thereafter he is brought up by grandparents, a delightful couple steeped in the simplest ideas of clan loyalty. By contrast, the three older brothers are allowed to run wild in the old MacDonald home, where they sleep with loaded rifles under their beds and piss joyfully out of the upstairs window. (The humble act of urination has an odd prominence throughout MacLeod's writing.) While Alexander is able to finish school and embark on a lucrative career, Calum and the others team up with their cousins and go to work in the mines.

From this point on, *No Great Mischief* becomes the story of three men with the same ancestral name. On the day that our Alexander MacDonald picks up his degree, he hears that his cousin and name-sake has been killed in the mine:

> I was probably having my picture taken when the bucket came down upon him. There was probably a mortar-board on my head in the instant when he had no head at all.

Partly out of guilt, Alexander agrees to take the dead man's place, to make up the numbers on a job. The chapters that follow are unsparing in their depiction of hard, dirty, dangerous work – while also honouring the pride and fellowship of the miners. When the clan is asked to take in a third Alexander MacDonald, a young man of whom they know nothing, they do so unquestioningly – and it is this act of trust that precipitates the novel's tragic climax.

In the end, the book passes a more critical verdict on the clannish-ness of the MacDonalds than we might expect. If loyalty to the tribe exerts an atavistic pull, it is also fraught with subtle forms of danger and deception. Regarded coolly, the episodes from Scottish history that are recounted with such pride tell a bleak enough tale – of loy-alty and stoicism repeatedly exploited, often by the Highlanders' own chiefs. The novel's title alludes to a remark made privately by General Wolfe, as his Highland troops prepared to lead the assault on Quebec: 'They are hardy, intrepid, accustomed to a rough country, and no great mischief if they fall.'

These are wide themes, and if their treatment never seems disem-bodied, it is a tribute to the intense physicality with which MacLeod renders his world. The stories are full of the most precise notations of climate, flora and fauna. Like Hardy, this was a man who 'noticed such things': the 'crashing muddied waves' of August, so different from those of autumn 'almost yellow at their peaks'; the distinction between the 'made ice' that forms in local seas and the 'drift ice' that comes down from the Arctic, with its grotesque forms and dazzling colours.

The extremity of the Cape Breton winter inspires some of MacLeod's most visceral writing. He describes days when walking into the wind makes 'your toes curl . . . within your shoes as if they are trying to grasp the earth' and you can feel the weight of the ice as it forms on your eyelashes. Clothes left out on the line 'creak . . . like sections of dismantled robots' and a dog sounds like castanets as its 'ice-coated hairs . . . clack together'. Some nights are so cold you can hear 'the trees exploding with the frost'.

The stories likewise evoke the teeming life of the island in spring and summer. The landscape flashes gold after rain, while bobolinks and red-winged blackbirds sing from the willows; the shadow of a hawk slides across grass as 'fat deer move among the rotting wind-fallen apples'. There is the time of trout 'battling and alive in the rushing, clear, cold water' and that of 'brown-dappled horses, rolling in the slickness of their summer fat'. The energies are often explicitly sexual, as with the August rams: 'Rearing and smashing against one another until their skulls thundered and reverberated like the growling icebergs of spring and their pent-up semen ejaculated in spurting jets . . .' The frank physicality of the language springs from a life lived in daily proximity to animals: MacLeod notices the 'sweet, heavy hotness' of a bull's grassy breath, the ears of an unborn calf 'exquisite and fragile and flatly pressed, like the memory of ferns found deep within the darkened earth'.

Elsewhere, there are scenes of ordinary life, often involving animals, which haunt like a picture from a favourite childhood book. One such is the sleigh ride in 'To Everything There Is a Season' – a magical flight through the cold and dark as 'snow from the horses' hooves falls about our heads like the whiteness of the stars'. *No Great Mischief* is packed with such things: those strangely powerful, almost heraldic tableaux in which the MacDonalds sit around the lamp at night with 'the huge brown heads of the horses against the window's frosted panes'. Best of all, perhaps, is the paradisal scene in which Calum is reunited with Christy, his old mare:

> All afternoon he lay on the warm grass offering her the bread and sugar cubes while she nuzzled his face . . . placing her great hooves carefully about the outline of his body . . . He sang to her in Gaelic . . . All day they stayed together on the green grass, giving and taking to and from each other.

As often in MacLeod, the language stands slightly sideways to the natural English idiom, but it has its own precisions, its shy and secret truths. That last phrase triggers the editor in me; shouldn't it be 'giving to and taking from'? Well, no. It's part of the absolute mutuality that MacLeod invokes here: in love we really do *give from* and *take to*; an insight at the heart and pith of his vision.

JONATHAN LAW is a writer and editor living in Buckinghamshire. His recent books include *The Whartons of Winchendon*, a short study of one of the strangest families in English history, featuring incest, treason, fairies, diving and the self-proclaimed Solar King of the World.

The Hunt for Hitler

ADAM SISMAN

I cannot now remember when I first read Hugh Trevor-Roper's *The Last Days of Hitler* (1947). My memory is confused by the fact that I knew the author in old age and was to become his biographer; Trevor-Roper himself told me about the extraordinary circumstances in which he had come to write the book. In September 1945 he had been awaiting discharge from the army so that he could resume his pre-war role as an Oxford don, when he was asked to undertake an urgent investigation into the fate of the Führer.

This was then a mystery. In January, as the Allied armies invaded Germany, Hitler had retreated to an underground bunker below the Reich Chancellery in Berlin, to escape Allied bombing; his last months would be spent in these eighteen small and windowless rooms. Towards the end, as the Russians moved ever closer, he would emerge only for a short stroll in the garden with his beloved Alsatian dog, until shelling made even this too dangerous. His subordinates had pleaded with him to leave Berlin while this was still possible, but he had chosen to stay. One of his final acts was to marry his devoted companion, Eva Braun. On 1 May his successor, Grand Admiral Dönitz, had announced in a solemn broadcast to the German people that the Führer had died fighting at the head of his troops. But Dönitz was far away in Schleswig-Holstein, and knew no more of what had happened to Hitler than he had been told in curt telegrams from the bunker.

In the months following the German surrender in May, rumours

Hugh Trevor-Roper, *The Last Days of Hitler* (1947)
Pan · Pb · 288pp · £9.99 · ISBN 9781447218616

spread that Hitler was still alive. He had escaped from besieged Berlin and was living on a mist-enshrouded island in the Baltic; in a Rhineland rock fortress; in a Spanish monastery; on a South American ranch; he had been spotted living rough among the bandits of Albania. A Swiss journalist made a deposition to testify that, to her certain knowledge, Hitler was living with Eva Braun on an estate in Bavaria. The Soviet news agency Tass reported that Hitler had been spotted in Dublin, disguised in women's clothing (perhaps his moustache had betrayed his identity). If anyone was in a position to know what had happened to him, it was the Russians, who had taken Berlin. But Stalin said that Hitler had escaped; and in the Soviet Union, what Stalin said outweighed evidence to the contrary.

The myth of Hitler remained potent. He had captured the imagination of the German people; so long as the possibility existed that he might still be alive, the stability and security of the occupied zones could not be guaranteed. This man had been responsible for the most destructive war in the history of the world, causing the deaths of tens of millions; the slightest chance that Hitler might return, as Napoleon had done, was too terrible to contemplate. The ghost haunting Europe had to be laid to rest. The uncertainty about Hitler's fate was poisoning the fragile relations between the victorious Allies. The Russians were now accusing the British of secretly harbouring him.

Trevor-Roper was entrusted with the hunt for Hitler. During the war he had shown himself to be an exceptionally able and determined intelligence officer. Now, though still only 31, he was given the authority of a major-general to undertake his inquiry, pursuing the evidence wherever it led. It was an extraordinary experience for a young historian, to be licensed to explore the ruins of a collapsed empire while the embers were still smoking. He would spend much of the next few weeks driving by jeep along empty German roads to interrogate potential witnesses. Sometimes he was driven by a young soldier, though often he was completely alone. At an early stage in his investigation he flew to Berlin to examine the bunker, now derelict and half-flooded, carelessly guarded by Russian soldiers.

The only conclusive proof that Hitler was dead would be the discovery and identification of his corpse. In the absence of a body, Trevor-Roper sought out those who had been with the Führer in the bunker at the end. Trevor-Roper was aware that his witnesses were fallible, especially when recalling events that had taken place five months earlier. They were particularly unreliable on dates; 'they could not possibly be otherwise, living as they did, perpetually underground, not distinguishing night from day, in circumstances of siege and bombardment'. He therefore relied on external sources to establish when events had taken place. He was a skilful and experienced interrogator, alert to inconsistencies and quick to detect when he was not being told the truth. By identifying and tracing a sufficient number of key witnesses, and confining his questioning to the essential facts, Trevor-Roper speedily accumulated enough evidence to establish an accurate narrative of Hitler's last weeks.

By early November Trevor-Roper was able to submit his report, 'The Death of Hitler', to the Quadripartite Intelligence Committee in Berlin. It concluded that Hitler had shot Eva Braun and then committed suicide by shooting himself on 30 April 1945, and that their bodies had subsequently been burnt. Goebbels had committed suicide the next day. Trevor-Roper was satisfied that the witnesses whom he had located and interrogated could not have combined to concoct a story robust enough to have withstood his questioning. 'The evidence from the sources at present available is entirely consistent in all material points, and this consistency is noteworthy since the groups of witnesses are quite independent of each other.' Trevor-Roper disposed crisply of alternative accounts of Hitler's fate. 'Other versions have been circulating suggesting that Hitler is not dead at all. These have been examined and found to rest on no valid evidence whatsoever.'

The report was enough to scotch the myth that Hitler had survived.

Hilary Paynter, *In Exile*, wood engraving based on the Hoffmann Garden
of the Jewish Museum, Berlin (detail)

But, as Trevor-Roper recognized, the subject provided an opportunity to write a book that would become a classic. Most works of contemporary history are quickly superseded as new evidence becomes available, but in this case the circumstances were exceptional, even unique.

> The theatre in which the action took place was closed; the actors were few and known; there were no seats for the public or the press; no reviews; no bulletins. The primary documents were few, and these were in my hands. Theoretically therefore the story could be told without fear of later correction.

Time has shown this theory to be correct. Trevor-Roper's *The Last Days of Hitler* remains in print, more than seventy years after its first publication; and though others have written on this subject subsequently, no one has significantly altered the picture first drawn by him.

The dramatic possibilities of a study of the last months of the Third Reich had occurred to Trevor-Roper the previous summer, when his interrogation of a captured German general had provided barely credible details of that disintegrating regime in all its exotic strangeness. Hess would only eat vegetables planted at full moon; Hitler was an insomniac, prone to such wild attacks of rage that he was known as *Teppich-beisser*, carpet-biter; at times he would lie on the floor and snap like a dog. Best of all was Göring, who now dressed completely in white silk: on his head he wore St Hubert's stag, with a swastika of gleaming pearls set between the antlers.

Trevor-Roper's subsequent inquiry into Hitler's fate had further fired his imagination. Stumbling down the dark steps and wading through the flooded passages and noisome, cell-like rooms of Hitler's bunker, he had been overwhelmed by a sense of terrible irony. An all-powerful tyrant, whose bullying had made ambassadors tremble, and whose oratory had electrified vast crowds at mass rallies, had passed his last weeks hiding underground in this squalid burrow, ranting to a dwindling entourage, and giving orders for the disposition of armies that had ceased to exist.

As he fingered the sodden, disintegrating papers that the Russians had unaccountably left undisturbed, Trevor-Roper identified the megalomaniac architectural plans that Hitler and Goebbels had studied together, while overhead the Russian shells rained down on their ruined capital, and the ground shook under the impact of their detonation.

And yet, however circumscribed, however insulated from reality, from the great events around it, the action in the bunker was somehow not trivial or parochial or irrelevant, for it symbolised and shadowed the greater drama outside: the drama of not a few days but of a whole generation.

The last days in this small shelter encapsulated 'the last convulsions of a European agony'. The Thousand-Year Reich had crumbled in a mere decade.

How could I fail to reflect on this nemesis of a pernicious ideology and the stupefying insolence of absolute power? What historian could fail to respond to such a challenge, such an opportunity? As for presentation, the situation itself was so dramatic, so bizarre, that it needed no rhetoric: it merely had to be set out.

The energy with which Trevor-Roper had pursued his investigation overflowed into his prose. He took as his starting point the 'July Plot' of 20 July 1944, when a group of middle-ranking army officers failed in their attempt to assassinate Hitler and overthrow the Nazi Party. This was followed soon after by the Allied breakout from Normandy, opening 'the last act in the tragedy of Germany'. The finale would be determined by the relentless advance of the Allied armies. Hitler's Germany contracted, pressed from each side by overwhelmingly superior forces, shrinking to a cramped, underground bunker. This was a story with its own dynamic, moving inexorably towards an apocalyptic end.

His wartime observations had convinced Trevor-Roper that 'the Nazi state was not (in any significant use of the word) totalitarian; and that its leading politicians were not a government but a court – a court as negligible in its power of ruling, as incalculable in its capacity for intrigue, as any oriental sultanate'. Far from being ruthlessly efficient, as Goebbels' propaganda had claimed and which many had swallowed, the Nazi state was in fact the opposite, for it contained no mechanism for self-criticism. The structure of German politics and administration, instead of being 'pyramidical' and 'monolithic', was 'a confusion of private empires, private armies, and private intelligence services'. Trevor-Roper depicted the leading Nazis as unscrupulous courtiers, greedily feasting off the spoils of conquest, jostling for favour, ever ready to belittle a rival and even, in the end, to abandon their leader. The story demanded a satirist: the characters were so absurd, their behaviour so grotesque, their ideology so horrible; only ridicule could touch them. Like the historian Tacitus, Trevor-Roper chronicled the death of a tyranny; and, like the satirist Juvenal, he skewered his victims by making them ludicrous.

The Last Days of Hitler became a bestseller. The royalty earnings enabled Trevor-Roper to buy a Bentley, which he parked ostentatiously in Tom Quad, the main quadrangle of his Oxford college, Christ Church. More significantly, it made him famous, and established his reputation as an expert on Nazi Germany, though his historical studies concentrated on the early seventeenth century. Indirectly it led to the great disaster of his life, his association with the forged Hitler Diaries. Thus one could say that Hitler made him; and Hitler unmade him. But that is another story, and now nobody under the age of 50 remembers the fiasco of the Hitler Diaries in 1983. *The Last Days of Hitler* remains an undiminished masterpiece.

ADAM SISMAN's biography of Hugh Trevor-Roper was published in 2010. He is now writing a book about a con man whom he discovered in Trevor-Roper's archive.

Man of Many Lives

MICHAEL HOLROYD

Does anyone today know who Frank Harris was? Are his novels and biographies read at all now? A hundred years ago he was acknowledged 'by all great men of letters of his time to be . . . greater than his contemporaries because he is a master of life', or so wrote the critic John Middleton Murry. George Meredith likened his novels to Balzac's, and Bernard Shaw his short stories to Maupassant's – high praise which was somewhat deflated by the discovery that one story had actually been lifted from Stendhal. But no one would have been more astonished at his disappearance as a great man of letters than Frank Harris himself. 'Christ goes deeper than I do,' he explained, 'but I have had wider experience.'

I first heard of Frank Harris from the biographer Hesketh Pearson. When he was young he had praised Harris as being 'the most dynamic writer alive'. This praise diminished over the years and Pearson never wrote a Life of Harris. But Harris made several comic appearances in my biographies. It was difficult to avoid him. There have been half a dozen published Lives of him and he makes many appearances in other writers' autobiographies. He seems also to have inspired several characters in works of fiction. Ford Madox Ford presented him in *The Simple Life Limited* (1911) as George Everard, 'his horrible unique self'. In Frederick Cassel's novel *The Adventures of John Johns* (1879) there is a caricature of him becoming editor of a newspaper by seducing the proprietor's wife. In George and Weedon Grossmith's

---

Hugh Kingsmill's *Frank Harris* (1932) is now out of print. However, we can obtain second-hand copies.

The Diary of a Nobody (1897) he appeared as Hardfur Huttle, 'a man who did all the talking' and came out with the most alarming ideas. H. G. Wells used him in his science-fiction novel *The War in the Air* (1907) as Butteridge, 'a man singularly free from false modesty' who believes 'all we have we owe to women'. It is surprising that a man with so many fictional lives seemed to disappear during the late twentieth century.

After his death, Harris came to life again in several dramatic roles. He appeared in the film *Cowboy* adapted in 1958 from his *My Reminiscences as a Cowboy*; then, in 1978, he could be seen in a BBC television play called *Fearless Frank*, played by Leonard Rossiter; and later in Tom Stoppard's theatre play *The Invention of Love*. His correspondence with Bernard Shaw was quietly published in 1982. Somehow and somewhere, his exploits were always available.

'The Connoisseur of Harris' was Hugh Kingsmill. In 1919 he published a novel called *The Will to Love* which he had written in a prisoner-of-war camp. Harris appears in it as Ralph Parker, a man whose friendship 'was a craving for an audience, his love, lust in fancy dress'. Yet 'in the ruins of his nature, crushed but not extinct, something genuine and noble struggled to express itself'. Harris was in his seventies when he died in the summer of 1931 and Kingsmill's biography of him was published the following year. They had known each other for twenty years and the book was one of those Lives that contain two main characters: the subject and the writer.

Kingsmill treats Harris as a comedian without a sense of humour. He seemed to be two different people, a Robin Hood who robbed the rich to help the poor – and a man determined not to be poor himself. He jettisoned one belief for another, longing for many things he did not want. A born actor was what he appeared to be, someone whose best performance was the noble art of seduction. 'His praise of sensuality', Kingsmill wrote, '. . . sounded melodiously in the ear of youth, and I hastened to sit at the feet of a master whose message agreed so well with what I desired from life.'

Harris's mother had died when he was 3 – and his sister was to instruct him how to attract girls and make a good marriage. Kingsmill described the rules as follows: 'First, praise the good points of the girl's face and figure; secondly, notice and approve her dress, for she will think you really like her if you notice her clothes; thirdly, tell her she is unique . . . and finally, kiss her.' To this Harris was to add 'the principle of feigned indifference'. He learnt all this so as to overcome his ugliness. 'I examined myself in a mirror, saw that I was ugly, and never looked at myself again.' His black hair

Frank Harris, *c.* 1922

was thick and low on his forehead, his features were irregular, he had large ears, an energetic chin and, worst of all, he was ridiculously short for a man of action. He tried to offset these disadvantages by developing his muscles until he resembled a prize-fighter. To gain an extra inch in height he used elevators in his boots, and to avoid his overtaxed digestion he made use of a stomach pump. His aim was to get pleasure and avoid its consequences – what Kingsmill described as 'to eat his cake and not have it'.

Harris did not understand that although men were attracted to women mainly by what they saw, women were more attracted to men by what they heard. Harris's attraction lay in his voice. He was endowed with a strong, dark, resonant, bass voice used with amazing fluency when he gave public speeches. To his young disciples he seemed the one man who could put the world to rights.

Frank, originally called 'James Thomas', had been born at one time or another during the 1850s, perhaps in Ireland, possibly in Wales – all depending on which of his autobiographical writings you read. Kingsmill did not hunt for certainties; he used Harris's escape from the storehouse of facts as a revelation of his character. 'He was born uneasy,' Kingsmill wrote. He hated his time at school where he was bullied by bigger boys and he did not get on well with his father. At the age of 14, with great courage and ingenuity, he set off for America to seek a happier life.

On reaching New York he became a bootblack, a workman in the caissons of Brooklyn Bridge and, arriving in Chicago, a night-clerk at a hotel where he joined a group of cowboys. Somehow his horsemanship enabled him to write on bull-fighting with the knowledge of an expert. He spent some time at Kansas University studying law and did not return to Europe until his very early twenties, travelling back by several routes. 'Harris travelling westwards across the Pacific and Harris travelling eastwards across the Atlantic met again in Paris,' Kingsmill explained.

Back in Britain he was to become the editor of several newspapers and magazines which gave him a prominent place in the literary scene. He began editing the *Evening News*, giving readers the suggestive and sensational stories he had enjoyed at the age of 14. Kingsmill quotes some of his headlines: 'Mad Dogs in the Metropolis', 'Measles in Church', 'Extraordinary Charge against a Clergyman', 'Awful Death in a Brewery'. He had the adroitness of a journalist and increased the sales of the papers he edited – *The Fortnightly Review*, the *Saturday Review* and *Modern Society*. But his downfall was sudden and as complete as his rise had been brilliant and unexpected. This was because he took no notice of what the proprietors wanted. He became discontented with reporting other people's happenings: he wanted to create happenings himself – especially political happenings. Adventures, he decided, came to the adventurous. He set about becoming a Tory Member of Parliament, marrying a wealthy widow who lived in Park Lane and entertaining politicians and businessmen – only to discover he thoroughly disliked them. He was a Tory, it is true, but he was also a socialist and an anarchist.

Kingsmill singled out three subjects of special interest among the biographies Harris wrote: Bernard Shaw, Oscar Wilde and Shakespeare. He wrote about Shaw at the end of his life and his biography was published posthumously. According to Shaw, Harris had 'an elaborate hypothesis of some fundamental weakness in my constitution' and it amused Shaw to counteract this with his generosity. Harris 'was grateful to Shaw for his unbroken friendliness', Kingsmill wrote, '. . . yet resentful at being helped by a man whose success exasperated him'. One of Shaw's most generous acts was to contribute a chapter to Harris's Life of Oscar Wilde.

Wilde had initially been repelled by Harris, while Harris was impressed by Wilde's charm, humour and social success. It was Harris who was to warn Wilde what would happen after Lord Queensberry had been acquitted of criminal libel. He urged Wilde to leave the country at once – a yacht was waiting for him in the Thames. But Wilde seems to have lost his nerve and was, as Harris predicted, found guilty of gross indecency and sent to jail for two years. Harris tried unsuccessfully to get well-known writers to sign a petition for his release and then visited Reading Gaol where he succeeded in getting him more humane conditions. And then he ruined their friendship. He took the plot of a play Wilde had planned and made it his own. He promised Wilde money when he was out of prison – and never gave it to him. And Wilde, who had been in tears at Harris's kindness, came to the conclusion that he 'has no feelings. It is the secret of his success.' Yet Harris had been brave: defending Wilde to the extent that he had to insist he himself was not homosexual – though, he added thoughtfully, 'if Shakespeare had asked me, I would have had to submit'.

Harris's *Oscar Wilde: His Life and Confessions* was published in 1916. *The Man Shakespeare and His Tragic Life Story* had come out after many years of writing and research seven years earlier. 'Frank Harris is upstairs,' Oscar Wilde had written, 'thinking about Shakespeare at the top of his voice.' It was probably his desire for fame that first prompted Harris to write about Shakespeare. On some pages he seems to confuse Shakespeare with himself. But his aim was to reveal the man behind the plays – the Victorians who studied the plays having forgotten there was such a man. He had read Georg Brandes's recent study of Shakespeare which he described as 'the ablest of Shakespeare's commentaries', though Kingsmill noted that he made 'no acknowledgement of his obvious debt to him'. Despite Harris's imperfections Kingsmill's book ends with his strengths.

> The finest passage in his writings is where he passes in review the spokesmen of Shakespeare's sadness or despair: Richard II sounding the shallow vanity of man's desires, the futility of man's hopes; Brutus taking an everlasting farewell of his friend and going willingly to his rest; Hamlet desiring unsentient death; Vincentio turning to sleep from life's deceptions; Lear with his shrieks of pain and pitiful ravings; Macbeth crying from the outer darkness.

> Kingsmill's biography is neither adulation nor an attack. Out of his candid recognition of weakness, Rebecca West wrote, 'there comes a living portrait which has made at least one reader who found Frank Harris's personality violently antipathetic understand why a great many people adored him and forgave him'.

MICHAEL HOLROYD's first book, politely turned down by fifteen publishers, was *Hugh Kingsmill* (1964).

On the Wings of History

KARIN ALTENBERG

I recently found myself in the excavated ruins of Stöng, a chieftain's farmhouse in the Icelandic valley of Þjórsárdalur. The manor, along with many neighbouring farms, was abandoned when the volcano Hekla erupted in 1104, covering this Icelandic Pompeii in pumice. Stöng is the best preserved early medieval farmhouse in the Nordic area, with massive turf walls still standing waist-high and a remarkable double-drained social lavatory, which would have accommodated a large gathering. In the main hall the cold slabs of the large central fireplace are visible and I was reminded of the appropriateness of the word 'window' – from the Old Norse *vindauga*, 'the eye of the wind' – where the smoke would escape through a single slit in the turf roof.

As I was standing there, imagining the densely walled, fire-lit hall, something stirred in me – a familiar sense of wonder and curiosity about the people who once made their lives here; who created culture in an unforgiving world, charged with the magic that stalked the borders between paganism and Christianity. An image formed in my imagination of a sleeping household, flea-ridden and night-barricaded against the battleaxe-wielding and torch-carrying neighbours of the Icelandic sagas, or perhaps against more unknown, Grendel-like monsters of the mind.

Kristin Lavransdatter, the Nobel Laureate Sigrid Undset's most celebrated work, brings the medieval North to life in an unparalleled

---

Sigrid Undset's trilogy *Kristin Lavransdatter* (1920–3) is out of print in English but we can obtain second-hand copies of a Penguin edition translated by Tiina Nunnally.

Hilary Paynter, *Turf Farm*, wood engraving (detail)

way. Set in fourteenth-century Norway the trilogy of novels was published between 1920 and 1923. Undset was awarded the Nobel Prize in 1928, and by then *Kristin Lavransdatter* had been translated into many languages and copies sold all over the world.

Born in 1882, Undset grew into a writer at a time when the 'New Woman' was starting to view life through the prism of her own being: through her intellect, her eroticism and her desires. She found support in her inner self, her 'woman's soul', rather than in social conventions and norms. Undset was trying to figure out how a woman could shape an independent life in a society formed by men, but, more importantly, she was also working out how to be a writer in this world. For this reason, Undset's protagonist Kristin Lavransdatter is not a maiden in a male epic but the artist of her own tragedy.

Like Undset, I have been fascinated by the early Middle Ages for as long as I can remember. Growing up as a self-sufficient and bookish child in a circumscribed village in southern Sweden I often felt cut out of another time. Merovingian, Visigoth and Viking were words of flux, feud, colour and turmoil that sent ripples through my being.

But even then I was wise enough not to let my enthusiasms and secret passions show.

My saving grace was my friend Axel, a perpetually tousled boy with dirty hands whose scent – a sandy, greeny blend – I can still recall, along with the eagerness of his breath as he spoke, although I have forgotten the sound of his voice. Between the ages of 4 and 12 we roamed together, exploring our slowly widening world. From our tree-house in Axel's parents' garden we planned each new pilgrimage; I conjured up the story and Axel, who was more practical, fashioned the paraphernalia: bows and arrows, a drawbridge and, one early summer evening when we were about 10, a 'decking of the hall' of the tree-house with roses, stolen from a local nursery, in order to make our little world beautiful. We often got into trouble.

As we ran through the local woods, armed with spears of birch, we were always prepared for danger. We promised to give each other a ship burial, should it come to it, but though we sensed strange and wonderful creatures in the undergrowth we never came across any actual monsters.

I had no notion then of being in any way different from Axel, but a few years later my first reading of *Kristin Lavransdatter* coincided with my being forced into a gender. My friendship with Axel was impossible by then; our naïve appetites were mocked in school and we knew that we would do better to ignore one another. *Kristin Lavransdatter* launched me on to the cusp of womanhood, manifesting my *self* through the kind of bewildered feminism that is the inevitable course for anyone who was once a tomboy and who has been expelled from that romance.

And so, in my early teens, I lost touch with Axel. Later I became a medieval archaeologist and a writer, if only to be able to continue to roam. That day in Iceland, being blown about by the wings of history in the ruined hall of Stöng, I had the notion that all my years were dissolving, like layers of skin, exposing for a moment the child who was once Axel's sister-in-arms with a crush on the Dark Ages.

This is why, I suppose, I decided to reread *Kristin Lavransdatter* last summer.

It is a 1,000-page novel of love, gender, class, marriage, family, work, honour, duty, ethics and faith, set in the most stunningly depicted emotional, political and natural landscape of southern Norway in 1302–49. As a child, Undset read *Njal's Saga* (see *SF* no. 39), which had a profound effect on her imagination and her linguistic sensitivity. The language of *Kristin Lavransdatter* reflects an Old Norse register of no-nonsense abruptness and wry stoicism while creating a literary pace of its own, allowing for lyrical – sometimes overwrought – descriptions of the interplay between nature and human sensibility and emotion.

Undset's father, an archaeologist, introduced her to the mindset and material culture of the Middle Ages, which gave her both a scientific approach to the study of the past and a keen eye for historical detail. And so, painstakingly, carefully painting with historical colour while never letting her research show, Undset re-imagined a credible medieval world where she could stage her own struggle as a woman at that time. She had previously written several contemporary novels but it was in her historical fiction, within the framework of a medieval world, that she could expand her re-imagining of a woman's life course. By the time she started writing *Kristin Lavransdatter*, she was a divorced mother of three young children. In 1924, after finishing the trilogy, she converted to Catholicism. Her concern with motherhood, her growing spirituality and anti-nihilism during this period are mirrored in Kristin's development.

Kristin Lavransdatter is a love story – but a masterly one that begins, in the first book of the trilogy, with Kristin swiftly breaking her society's norms of patriarchy, duty and honour in order to give herself over to erotic passion. Undset viewed eroticism – a desire so profound that life would be intolerable if it were not satisfied – as part of the spiritual sphere. Kristin falls, in every way, for the handsome but clearly unsuitable Erlend Nikulaussøn, although her father has already pledged her to the thoroughly decent Simon Darre. When the wedding between Kristin and Erlend is finally allowed to happen, at the end of the first book, it is an excruciating affair, the bridal crown weighing so heavily on Kristin's head that she can hardly sit upright at the banquet.

The second book would delight any agony aunt who recommends 'working things out' in a relationship. For Kristin it is about coming to terms with the life that she has chosen for herself. In the last book, after a stubborn battle of wills with Erlend, she finally kicks him out. Although the reader is often tempted to question Erlend's character and values, we never doubt Kristin's love for him – to her he does not have to be the best man, her loving him is enough. And it is clear that Erlend, in a patriarchal world, treats Kristin as his equal, which may not always make for great romance. After Erlend's death (speared in the groin, defending her honour), she retreats to a convent, seeking forgiveness, and dies in the Black Death.

I do the trilogy an injustice by trying to summarize it because the delight of these books is not the plot – though as plots go it is lively enough – but rather the universal truths of love between parents and children, friends and lovers. Kristin is a complex, flawed and entirely believable individual with extraordinary dignity and integrity. To get to know her is to understand the nature of love and the workings of human relationships over time. Thankfully, Undset is not didactic. If anything, she shows the reader that to be human means understanding that there is always more than one way to live a life, to love, to be part of a family or a religion. However, to understand this, one has to give in to life, as Fru Aashild, Erland's kinswoman, explains to Kristin:

> I'm not foolish enough to complain because I have to be content with sour, watered-down milk now that I've drunk up all my wine and ale. Good days can last a long time if one tends to things with care and caution; all sensible people know that.

That's why I think that sensible people have to be satisfied with the good days – for the grandest of days are costly indeed.

But there is another aspect to this work, which made my teenage self devour these pages. This has to do with history and fiction – and with historical fiction. Faced with the threat of reality in a place where nothing seemed to happen (unless Axel and I created our own history), Kristin's story mystified the reality of adulthood, which I was inevitably entering, and rendered it interesting. Like any great historical novelist Undset showed the reader that people in the past were like us – it is just the circumstances of society that change. And so the inquiry into other worlds may help us to widen the narrow circumstances of our own lives, our particular reality, by encompassing a shared humanity.

KARIN ALTENBERG is currently writing a novel set in a time and place she knows little about. As a result she's trying very hard to live in the present, knowing that the good old days never really happened.

Murder Most English

JANET WALKINSHAW

Recently, getting to know the new man in my life, I was browsing through his bookshelves and discovered he had all twelve of the Flaxborough novels. I knew instantly this man was for me, at least for the length of time it took me to reread these old favourites.

Colin Watson's first crime novel set in the vaguely Lincolnshire market town of Flaxborough, *Coffin, Scarcely Used,* was published in 1959, the last, *Whatever's Been Going on at Mumblesby?* in 1982 shortly before his death. A 1969 omnibus edition of the first three novels has endpapers that show a bird's-eye view sketch of the town. There is the river, into which a body was tipped in 1972. There is Heston Lane where dwelt several of the town's most respectable citizens until their sudden unexpected demise. There is Market Place, locus of the Friday market where in 1979 a carelessly driven car hit Constable Cowdrey as he was awaiting delivery under the counter of a pound of sausages. There also in 1977 did Robert Digby Tring meet his end by falling through the inexplicably unlatched door of a fairground ride, forty feet up in the air. And there is Jubilee Park where the drinking

---

Colin Watson's twelve Flaxborough novels are: *Coffin, Scarcely Used* (1958); *Bump in the Night* (1960); *Hopjoy Was Here* (1962); *Lonelyheart 4122* (1967); *Charity Ends at Home* (1968); *The Flaxborough Crab* (1969); *Broomsticks over Flaxborough* (1972); *The Naked Nuns* (1975); *One Man's Meat* (1977); *Blue Murder* (1979); *Plaster Sinners* (1980); and *Whatever's Been Going on at Mumblesby?* (1982). There have been several editions of them, some with different titles for the American market. They are currently available as print-on-demand Faber Finds or we can source second-hand copies.

fountain erected to the memory of Lt.-Col. William Courtney-Snell JP was the meeting place of Lonelyheart 4122 and Lonelyheart 347 in 1967 and which several years later was blown up as a prelude to murder.

It isn't quite the closed community of the Golden Age of Crime Fiction, but this town of 15,000 inhabitants is far enough from any city to form a world of its own, with a hinterland of seedy farms and questionable manufactures. Here live Justin Scorpe, lawyer; Barrington Hoole, optician; Leonard Leaper, cub reporter turned fanatical pastor. Walter Grope, commissionaire at the Rialto cinema, composes verse while herding the queues: 'The river winds and winds and winds,/ through scenery of many kinds'. On retirement he earns money writing 'In Memoriam' notices. Dozens of other fellow citizens weave in and out of the novels, here as a witness, there as a subplot, and now and again they commit murder. As well then that there, in the centre of town, in Fen Street, is the Police Station.

Presiding over all is Inspector Purbright, a large unassuming man with a bland pleasant face beneath corn-coloured hair. Like all the best detectives he is keenly interested in irrelevancies and gossip, particularly that of fat Sergeant Malley, Coroner's Officer, who knows everyone and everything. There is nothing angst-ridden about Purbright: he's not divorced; he's not an alcoholic; he gardens. He lives peaceably at 33 Tetford Drive with his wife Ann with whom he goes shopping on Saturday mornings. He is the quintessentially quiet Englishman, competent at his job, in which we suspect he finds some amusement. Such is his unfailing courtesy that no one, not his Chief Constable, nor his subordinates (one of whom calls him Sarky), can ever be sure whether he is secretly laughing at them or not.

Purbright is ably assisted by Detective Sergeant Sidney Love, possessed of an innocent choir-boy face and a certain innocence of mind to go with it. But not as innocent as the mind of Chief Constable Harcourt Chubb, a breeder of Yorkshire terriers and geraniums, who never sits down but always leans, on mantelpieces, filing cabinets, desks. He has difficulty understanding that there are people of nefarious intent in the world: '"Not Flaxborough people surely." There was a note of pleading in Mr Chubb's voice' (*Coffin, Scarcely Used*).

Above all there is Miss (always Miss) Lucilla Edith Cavell Teatime, who wanders into Flaxborough in *Lonelyheart 4122* and stays for eight more novels. She is a well-dressed woman of a certain age, and we know little of her previous history. She claims an upbringing in the Rectory, and I for one believe her. She once lived in Twickenham. The name Harrods is best not mentioned in her presence. On arrival in Flaxborough she finds it charming.

'I do like the sea of course. Do you not find Flaxborough smells of the sea?'

'We have a tidal river . . . And there are docks.'

'I am very fond of docks. Not', she added dreamily, 'that I have ever been in one, you understand.'

Not marked on the map but easily located by the steeple of the church of St Lawrence is Church Close and the narrow Georgian house where she lives in dove-grey elegance. Her pursuits are various. Here she is the proprietor of a herb farm with only one product, Lucky Fen Wort ('for Vitality and Improvement of Natural Functions'). There we meet her as the owner of the House of Yesteryear, selling antiques. In *Broomsticks over Flaxborough* she finds it expedient to be Operational Director of the Edith Cavell Psychical Research Foundation:

'Edith Cavell?'

Miss Teatime blushed. 'My middle names actually. Rather shame-making but the Trust insisted. They meant it kindly, I suppose, but people do not realize how unworthy of them is this persistent deference to money and aristocratic connection.'

But most of the time she is Secretary of the Flaxborough & Eastern Counties Charities Alliance. And charity for Miss Teatime begins at home. She is often one step ahead of Inspector Purbright in solving the crime but a Miss Marple she is not. If you visit her you will be served afternoon tea in the finest of bone-china cups. If you are an old friend you will be offered a slug of whisky to put in it. She will light up one of her cheroots.

From the first paragraph of each of these novels you know you are in the hands of a master. The humour is wry, dry, occasionally surreal, frequently laugh-out-loud, but it never tips over into whimsy. The plots and counterplots, double-crosses and crossed wires border on the absurd but never lose sight of the basic requirements of a crime novel: a body, a murder weapon, a motive, an investigation and an arrest. There are the side-achingly funny set pieces: the Extraordinary General Meeting of the local witches' coven, with chairwoman, secretary and Warlock Parkin making tedious points of order, while Mrs Gooding just wants to get her clothes off; the reluctant summer outing of the residents of Twilight Close; the visit to a barber by a spymaster in search of a lost agent. Scenes like these are to be savoured. It is Colin Watson's skill that we, the readers, are privy to much that is hidden from the police but we can still be surprised by the dénouement. And it is his witty writing which makes us reread the novels time and again even though we know the outcome.

Colin Watson was born in 1920. At the age of 17 he was appointed as a junior reporter on a Boston newspaper, and he spent his working life in Lincolnshire, latterly writing editorials for a chain of newspapers. He was a member of the Detection Club of Great Britain and he won the CWA Silver Dagger twice. In his photos, bespectacled, moustached, he looks like one of his own creations, a quiet, reserved Englishman, and by all accounts that is what he was. Who knew that he could see, under the bland surface of a quiet country town, the joyous anarchy of the ordinary citizen's life? And if he couldn't see it, he could invent it, and describe it in what must be some of the most elegant language of any crime novel.

Watson also wrote two non-fiction books: *Puritan* (1966) and *Snobbery with Violence* (1971). The latter is a study of the English class attitudes that informed the crime novels and thrillers of the late nineteenth and early twentieth centuries. Sometimes, in his Flaxborough novels, he deliberately nods in the direction of these earlier writers, with irony and, dare I say it, some affection. He died at the age of 63 and is buried in the churchyard at Folkingham in Lincolnshire. On his tombstone is noted his profession – 'Author'.

JANET WALKINSHAW lives in south-west Scotland. She has written three novels set during the Scottish Reformation: *Knox's Wife*, *The Five-year Queen* and *Lochleven*. Her article was a runner-up in our 2018 Writers' Competition.

Love and Loss in Brussels

HELEN MACEWAN

In 2016, in a debate organized by the Brontë Society, a panel of four writers discussed the relative merits of *Jane Eyre* (see *SF* no. 40) and Charlotte Brontë's last novel, *Villette*. When an audience vote was taken, the earlier and better-known book won, but only by a small majority; the two writers defending *Villette* had been eloquent in its praise. As one of them said, you often come to appreciate it later in life. If *Jane Eyre* is *Pride and Prejudice*, *Villette* is *Persuasion*.

The general reading public has always voted unequivocally for the bestselling *Jane Eyre*. Not only is *Villette* a darker book, but the popular image of the Brontës does not readily associate them with a continental girls' boarding school. And I must admit that *Villette's* heroine Lucy Snowe initially failed to engage me, perhaps because I was too young when I first read it.

Charlotte's publisher George Smith, who had brought her fame overnight with *Jane Eyre*, had his own doubts about *Villette* when he received the manuscript. For one thing, he feared that readers would take a dim view of Lucy for being in love with two men: halfway through the book she transfers her affections from the handsome young Englishman Graham Bretton to Paul Emmanuel ('Monsieur Paul'), a fellow-teacher at Madame Beck's Pensionnat in the town of Villette.

One aspect Smith did not comment on, however, but which can hardly have escaped his notice was that Graham Bretton was closely

Charlotte Brontë, *Villette* (1853)
Penguin · Hb · 672pp · £14.99 · ISBN 9780241198964

modelled on himself. For a time, the 36-year-old Charlotte was attracted to her charming young publisher, who was her host on her trips to London.

Did she feel any discomfort at the thought that as Smith read the manuscript he was also reading her feelings about him (including her astute assessment of his limitations)? We don't know, but we do know that she had a history of drawing heavily on real people and places in her fiction. For the cast of *Shirley*, written between *Jane Eyre* and *Villette*, she took inspiration from local curates, the family of an old schoolfriend and her sister Emily. In *Villette*, for the character of the schoolmaster in whom Lucy Snowe finds a soulmate Charlotte looked no further than the Belgian schoolteacher who had tutored her during her stay in Brussels some years earlier, in 1842–3: Constantin Heger, the man with whom she became infatuated.

More than that, she put into *Villette* just about every element of her two years at the Pensionnat Heger, run by Zoë Heger with help from her husband Constantin. Charlotte went there, with Emily, to study French, but ended up also teaching English to pay for her keep. The teaching was a trial, but French literature tutorials with Heger were intoxicating. Without actually naming Brussels and Belgium as such in the novel (Brussels becomes Villette, 'little town', and Belgium Labassecour, 'the farmyard'), she poured into it her contempt for Belgian schoolgirls (referred to as the 'swinish multitude'); her dislike of Mme Heger, whose personality suggested at least some traits of Mme Beck, Lucy Snowe's formidable employer; and her intense feelings for Constantin Heger, transformed into the volatile M. Paul.

There is no lack of fun and vivacity in the book, but the sombre mood of its most moving passages reflects that of Charlotte in her second year in Brussels, when she returned without Emily. She was homesick and saw less and less of Heger, who had been the main reason for her return. Remaining alone at the school in the long vacation, she fell into a depression. Back home in Yorkshire a few

The Pensionnat Heger garden, which inspired the school garden in *Villette*, from a sketch by a visitor which appeared in *Harper's Monthly* in August 1858

months later, she spilled out her longing for Heger in letters to him that went largely unanswered.

An unsatisfied craving for love, solitude, depression: constants throughout Charlotte's life, they came to a head in Brussels. Moreover, *Villette* was written, almost a decade after the Brussels experience, at a time when Charlotte was once again, to use a phrase of our day, 'in a dark place'. The success of *Jane Eyre* and *Wuthering Heights* in 1847 had been closely followed by the death of all three of her siblings. Alone at Haworth Parsonage with her elderly father, she was facing a future as a lonely woman as well as a single one.

My second reading of *Villette* took place at the stage of life when *Persuasion* starts to strike chords. Besides this, by now I was familiar with Charlotte's biography. Not that any biographical knowledge is necessary for a full appreciation of *Villette*. We readers know we must be wary of reading fiction as the author's life. Lucy Snowe wasn't Charlotte Brontë in all respects any more than M. Paul was M. Heger. Even so, *Villette* is the most autobiographical of Charlotte's novels.

By the time she wrote it, she had quite a lot more emotional experience to draw on, much of it painful, than when she dashed off *Jane Eyre* at white heat, in a few months, at the age of 30. But for the *mise en scène* of this work of her maturity she went back in time to the foreign adventure on which she'd embarked with such youthful hopefulness.

The Brontës' novels and their passionate protagonists are generally associated with the open moors, but an urban backdrop and the claustrophobia of a Brussels boarding school form a powerful setting for Lucy Snowe's inner drama. Charlotte complained of Haworth as a remote spot where she felt cut off; life was going on somewhere else, passing her by. In Brussels she knew what it was to live in a city yet spoke of being 'isolated in the midst of numbers', lonely in the heart of a capital. Not only was she usually cooped up in the classroom, but the Hegers' school lay in a quiet enclave just below and removed from the bustle of the royal quarter. As does Mme Beck's. In her solitary hours of leisure Lucy can hear the rumble of carriages on their way to ballrooms and theatres. Occasionally she ventures out into that brightly lit world of concerts and plays with Graham Bretton, but mostly she is confined within the school walls.

In winter I sought the long classes, and paced them fast to keep myself warm . . . In summer it was never quite dark, and then I went upstairs to my own quarter of the long dormitory, opened my own casement . . . and leaning out, looked forth upon the city beyond the garden, and listened to band-music from the park or the palace-square, thinking meantime my own thoughts, living my own life in my own still, shadow-world.

At times, this shadow-world becomes a very dark and lonely place indeed. Alone at the Pensionnat in the summer vacation, Lucy starts hallucinating, seeing 'the ghastly white beds . . . turning into spectres' in the deserted dormitory. In this state of mind, she is tormented by the 'insufferable thought' that she is not loved. In the long weeks of the summer of 1843, Charlotte suffered a virtual nervous breakdown. But Lucy's descent into hell drew on more than this Brussels experience. On sleepless nights at the Parsonage in the years after the death of her sisters, Charlotte seemed to hear their voices in the wind, crying to be let in. And the fear of meeting loved ones after death only to find them changed and indifferent towards her was one that haunted her.

That summer in Brussels, Charlotte, the daughter of a Protestant pastor, was prompted by despair to persuade a Catholic priest in the cathedral to hear her confession, writing to Emily: 'I took a fancy to change myself into a Catholic and go and make a real confession to see what it was like.' The episode provided one of the most highly charged in *Villette*.

> Any opening for appeal to God was as welcome to me then as bread to one in extremity of want. I knelt down with others on the stone pavement. It was an old solemn church, its pervading gloom not gilded but purpled by light shed through stained glass . . . The priest within the confessional . . . quietly inclined his ear to my lips . . .

Lucy's opening words to the priest are the very ones spoken by Charlotte in St Gudule's in Brussels: '*Mon père, je suis protestante.*'

This priest turns up later as M. Paul's own confessor, Père Silas, who keeps a suspicious watch on his growing friendship with the Protestant Lucy and takes care to inform her of M. Paul's fidelity to the memory of his early love, who died soon after taking the veil when their marriage was forbidden.

Mme Beck's Pensionnat and the Catholic city of Villette, with their stories of nuns and their spying, omnipresent priests, are as Gothic in their way as Thornfield Hall. The real Pensionnat was on ground formerly owned by a guild of archers; a half-buried slab in its garden was said to conceal the entrance to an underground passage, an escape route in times of siege. The fictional school in *Villette* has formerly been a convent. It still has a resident nun, or rather the ghost of one. Legend has it that a slab in the garden is 'the portal of a vault, imprisoning . . . the bones of a girl whom a monkish conclave of the drear middle ages had here buried alive for some sin against her vow'. This spectral nun is sighted by Lucy at moments of crisis – as when she buries her letters from Graham Bretton who, she knows, will never have more than friendly feelings for her.

'You are good, you are beautiful; but you are not mine,' she tells him mentally after interring the letters at the foot of Methuselah, the ancient pear tree. In Haworth, letters were Charlotte's link with the outside world. Those from Heger and, later, George Smith were also food for her emotional hunger, and days waiting for them were days of starvation. Heger stopped writing, and tore up her frantic appeals to him (stitched back together by his wife, they can be seen today in the British Library); George Smith married someone younger, prettier and richer than her. Graham Bretton marries exquisite, fairy-like Paulina, but Lucy likes to think that a 'little closet' in his heart is reserved for 'quiet Lucy Snowe'.

The novel reverses the chronological order of the two relationships that informed it. Charlotte's infatuation with Heger came years before her flirtatious friendship with Smith, but in *Villette*, after the symbolic burial of her love for Graham in the walled garden, Lucy soon finds herself, on summer evenings, deep in conversation in its *allées* with her irascible colleague M. Paul. As friendship flowers into love, Mme Beck's garden becomes as enchanted a spot as Thornfield

Hall's, the scent of M. Paul's cigar in the evening air as heady as Mr Rochester's.

There's no mad wife in an attic to keep them apart, and M. Paul's long-lost first love turns out to be no impediment after all. But unlike *Jane Eyre*, *Villette* offers no happy ever after. In the three years of M. Paul's absence overseas, however, before the storm at sea that closes the book, letters once again provide nourishment. Those Lucy receives from him, she tells us, made those three years 'the happiest of her life'.

Like Lucy, Charlotte briefly found happiness, in her case in marriage at the age of 38 to an unlikely-seeming suitor, her father's curate. She died in pregnancy nine months later.

Lucy successfully runs her own school and lives on until her hair is white under her cap, 'like snow beneath snow'. Charlotte didn't even make it to her thirty-ninth birthday, but in spirit, like Lucy, she was a survivor. She put into *Villette* not just her pain but the qualities that fortified her to soldier on through loneliness and loss.

HELEN MACEWAN is a translator and former teacher who lives in Brussels. Her books include *The Brontës' Brussels*, an illustrated guide to Charlotte and Emily Brontë's time in the Belgian capital, and *Through Belgian Eyes: Charlotte Brontë's Troubled Brussels Legacy.*

Oh Nancy, Nancy!

SAM LEITH

When I was 4, I fell in love for the first time. The object
of my affections was Jemima the rag-doll from *Play
School*. That was a trial run. I was 7 or 8 when I got my
first serious crush. She was an older woman: red-haired,
wholesome, adventurous and intelligent. She was 16. She
was always 16. Her name was Nancy. My love for her –
like the young Julian Barnes's love for an older woman
– did a great deal to shape my life.

The Nancy Drew mysteries (I didn't know, then, that 'mystery' is
what Americans call a detective story) were the first series of books to
which I became completely addicted. And, since there were dozens
of them, it seemed as if I could never run out – useful, for a child
who weekly exhausted his borrowing limit at Dorking Library.

My grandfather got into the habit, for a bit, of buying me one a
week. Whenever I had a book token, it was into the bookshop at the
top of the main street (I can't for the life of me remember its name)
that I would go. Oh! the anticipation of a fresh one, a fresh mystery,
smelling of new paperback, picked off the long shelf of Nancy Drew
books in the children's section and taken home in a crisp paper bag.

That long shelf was itself a part of the pleasure. I grew a long shelf
of my own. Before I piqued myself on my row of white-spined
Picador books in my teens, or the black-spined battalion of Penguin

---

There are a great many Nancy Drew mysteries available as new paperbacks or as
second-hand copies. For a full list of titles and dates of publication see the
Wikipedia entry for Nancy Drew.

Classics (a purple stripe across the top for Latin or Greek; red for English; yellow for Russian or French; and the odd showy green if you had the *Bhagavad Gita*), my pride was in a lengthening collection of uniform Nancy Drew mysteries, filed in numerical order. It was a great long stripe of primrose.

The editions matter, the physical books matter, when you're reading with that intensity: they are part of the memory. This was when Armada was publishing them in the UK in a uniform design that one collector I've found online has called the 'yellow box' editions. The covers were a soft yellow – not far off the colour of *Slightly Foxed*, though a wee bit yellower – with a painted illustration in a box on the front below the author and title. All those illustrations, it seems, were the work of one Peter Archer. A triangle of colour on the bottom left corner, matching the colour of the title, told you that this was 'Nancy Drew Mystery No. . . . .'.

Oddly, one of the very first I read – *The Mystery of the Tolling Bell* – was different. It had a white cover with a photograph of a startled-looking Nancy, rather than a painting, and a brassier design-scheme: the author's name picked out in typewriter-style Courier and the title in crisp blue block capitals. The flash said, 'As seen on TV', though I don't remember ever seeing her on TV.

My Nancy Drew years can be dated. Google tells me that these editions were in print from 1975 to 1982. I was born in 1974. I must have caught the tail end of the yellow-box editions – and, indeed, I remember a faint sense of unease and disapproval when they started to appear in a new guise. They were a different colour, with rather trashy painted images spilling out of a circle in the centre of the cover, and a 'Nancy Drew' logo in blockbuster size above, in star-spangled Country-and-Western lettering, dwarfing title and author. Those editions were the beginning of the end of my time with Nancy. We were starting to grow apart.

Still, the titles alone are a waft of literary Bisto. *The Secret of the Old Clock. Nancy's Mysterious Letter. The Clue in the Crossword Cipher.*

The Clue in the Crumbling Wall. The Whispering Statue. Each one was a mystery, a secret, a clue, a quest, a password, a ghost. The stories, like those of Scooby-Doo, existed in a world that was laced with the supernatural, or the suggestion of it, but that always (as far as I remember) provided naturalistic, human explanations. They were spooky but reassuring; domestic gothic.

Nancy was what would – when the books were written, between the '30s and the '70s – have been called 'spunky': she was *intrepid*. She sneaked about finding clues, and she braved and faced down dangers and villainy. Hers was a bounded world – bounded not only by its familiar human furniture (widowed father, housekeeper, cousins George and Bess, chaste boyfriend Ned) but, as I can now see too, by the world of WASP privilege she inhabited.

And the stories were exciting. They were exciting enough that they occasioned my 'sneak reading' – after-lights-out marathons, for the most part shrewdly tolerated by my parents, which unless I'm misremembering them really did involve torches under the covers as per the cliché. And I recall clearly once literally bouncing up and down on my bed exclaiming 'Nancy! Nancy!' in excitement and alarm, she having found herself in a situation that would now be described by the British Board of Film Classification as containing 'mild peril'.

Nancy Drew's adventures would be supplanted, in time, by the works of Wilbur Smith and Stephen King, Hammond Innes and James Michener, with eye-widening peeks into the Harold Robbins on my parents' shelves – giants of the '70s, many now belonging to the fossil record.

And they were not all I read, even then: I also adored the 'Adventure' series by Willard Price, which told the stories of Hal and Roger Hunt, teen zoologists who travelled the world having encounters with animals; and the Doctor Who novelizations by Terrance Dicks. I read Malcolm Saville's Lone Pine series; and the Three Investigators books, which came with the endorsement of no less than Alfred Hitchcock. But the Nancy Drew books were first among equals.

And even then, I was forming the beginnings of what – for a future professional book reviewer – I fancied was literary discrimination. For instance, I might have enjoyed the Three Investigators but I had no truck with the Famous Five: Enid Blyton did nothing whatever for me.

Of one thing I was absolutely certain: Nancy Drew was an infinitely superior product to the Hardy Boys. Carolyn Keene, the author of the former, was in every respect a better stylist and storyteller than Franklin W. Dixon, who wrote those adventures. Oh, the blandness of the Hardy Boys, with their bluff blond extrovert masculinity, their letter-sweater squareness. Nancy – motherless Nancy, mystery-tangled, feminine, solitary, clever Nancy – was something altogether other.

Here, I'm afraid, was my fundamental error. For Carolyn Keene never existed. And nor did Franklin W. Dixon. And inasmuch as they did exist, they were the same person: the collective pen-name of an East Coast writing syndicate founded by Edward Stratemeyer (1862–1930). Peter Archer painted the Hardy Boys covers too, though I never noticed. Nancy was a factory product. Of Stratemeyer, who sold 500 million books even though you've never heard of him, it was said: 'As oil had its Rockefeller, literature had its Stratemeyer.'

He died in the year that Nancy first appeared in print – though he wrote the outline for the first three novels. In her world, Nancy has a living father but a dead mother; in the real world she had a dead father but a living mother. Of the dozens of ghostwriters who produced the stories between 1930 and the present day, Mildred Wirt Benson (1905–2002) was the queen. She lived in Toledo, Ohio, and was paid a flat fee of between $125 and $250 for each book. And she wrote most of the ones I so delighted in – all but seven of the first thirty books in the series. Here was, as I never knew at the time, *The Mystery of the Invisible Ghost*.

We have ghostwriters to this day. But the writing syndicate – a huge yet under-noticed feature of twentieth-century publishing – seems to have gone the way of all flesh. And that may seem, to most literary sensibilities, like a good thing – the demise of a conveyor-belt approach to fiction-writing as product, to art as so many tins of beans. But to quote George Eliot, 'that things are not so ill with you and me as they might have been, is half owing to the number who lived faithfully a hidden life, and rest in unvisited tombs'. The Stratemeyer syndicate – and Mildred Wirt Benson, resting in her unvisited tomb – brought Nancy Drew to me, and my 8-year-old life was incomparably richer as a result.

I think I was 10 or 11 when, for my younger brother's birthday, I gave him my complete collection of Nancy Drew novels. I remember the weight of them, held between my two hands like a squeezebox. Not a cheap hand-me-down. As he knew, I was giving him the most precious thing I owned. I don't think he ever read them.

The franchise goes on. Feminist literary theorists study them. Hillary Clinton and Laura Bush have cited them as influences. They've changed publishers and formats. Nancy has been reinvented as an 18-year-old with a mobile phone and an environmentally friendly electric car. Wikipedia tells me they've sold 80 million copies in 45 languages, spawned five films, two television series and a number of video games.

But all that seems irrelevant. I'll always have my Nancy: the one who appeared in yellow Armada paperbacks between 1979 and 1982.

SAM LEITH is the literary editor of the *Spectator* and the author of *You Talkin' to Me? Rhetoric from Aristotle to Obama* and *Write to the Point: How to be Clear, Correct and Persuasive on the Page*.

Striking Sparks

DEREK PARKER

Not until long after the dust had settled did I realize that the Battle of Earls Court Square, in which I played a significant role, had been preceded twenty years earlier by the Battle of Portman Square.

The ancient commander who lived through both skirmishes, Chevalier Galloway Kyle – the founder of the Poetry Society – could have told me all; but in his nineties he claimed to remember nothing. He had edited the *Poetry Review*, the Society's magazine, from 1916 until 1947, when he handed it over to a pretty blonde 27-year-old Scot called Muriel Spark, who was offered the position of Editor solely because she had won first prize in the Society's competition for a love lyric with – she confessed – a sonnet cold-bloodedly composed in a style she thought would impress the judges. The prize – two guineas – was important to an impecunious writer, as was the offer, with the post, of a free flat in Portman Square. That, for Spark, was a clincher. Alas, she never moved in – the first of a number of unpleasant surprises.

Even before the publication of her first issue, Spark was in trouble with members of the Society's Executive Committee. She insisted that the poems she published should be paid for: an unheard-of and revolutionary suggestion. The honour should surely be sufficient? Then, her first editorial began 'Cannot we cease railing against the moderns?' This was to suggest that her readers should be divested of a distinctive pleasure. The moment she began serious work, there was trouble with former contributors who found their submissions returned. A Miss Alice Hunt Bartlett of New York was puzzled and alarmed when her verses were rejected. She had never had any trouble with the previous editor, who had never failed either to publish her or to cash the cheque for $25 which always accompanied her submissions. Other former regular contributors wrote protesting letters, though unaccompanied by either cheques or cash.

The most active member of the Executive Committee was Robert Armstrong. Spark published in her first issue a poem of his which had been accepted by the previous editor but failed to print his name on the magazine's cover. He complained bitterly, in a letter on Civil Service notepaper which bore his title: Inspector of Taxes (Willesden District). He said that he was a well-known contributor to prominent Civil Service journals under such names as 'Critic', 'Observer' and 'Dunrobin Goodfellow': it was a surprise to find himself listed among the 'other contributors' rather than by name. He had been working hard 'to put the Society and yourself on the map', putting in 'some groundwork with influential friends', and to find himself so unrecognized was 'a surprise'.

Spark made the mistake of replying that if his only literary contributions had been published under pseudonyms, she did not consider that the absence of his name was necessarily a special loss to readers. She thus made a bitter enemy, and it seemed entirely possible that he was the source of a number of anonymous letters which began to appear, addressed to 'The Editor', and complaining desperately about everything to do with the *Review*.

Armstrong engaged a number of lieutenants, prominent among them the editor of *Birth Control News*, Dr Marie Stopes, one of the Society's Vice-Presidents, and the intimate friend until his recent death of Lord Alfred Douglas (Wilde's 'Bosie'). She published scurrilous rumours about Spark's private life, appearing at general meetings shrieking and shaking her fists. William Kean Seymour, who had wanted to be Editor, and who had done everything he could to obstruct Spark from the beginning, accused her of holding 'underground meetings' (for what purpose he did not reveal). Armstrong began 'editing' poems by obtaining proofs from the printers without the

Editor's knowledge and reported Spark to the Committee for writing letters to 'her supporters' on the magazine's notepaper (his own were invariably written on Inland Revenue stationery). Meanwhile what seemed almost innumerable rejected poets wrote protesting letters to Lord David Cecil, the Society's President, who tore them up.

Spark battled on for two years then left, exhausted by the continual slow drip of opposition, sometimes swelling to a torrent. Pressed by the Council to resign, she chose to be dismissed, which meant she was at least then entitled to three months' severance pay. Readers of her 1981 novel *Loitering with Intent* – in which the heroine works for the Autobiographical Association – will find a few incidents unmistakably derived from the Battle of Portman Square.

Eighteen years later, on the basis of two slim – and I mean *slim* – collections of poems, I was suggested as a possible editor of the *Poetry Review* by its then Editor, John Smith. Had Muriel Spark's memoir *Curriculum Vitae* been published in 1966 rather than 1992 I might well have thought twice before accepting the unpaid position. But as it was, I had no premonition of trouble at Smith's introduction: 'And this is the General Secretary of the Society – Robert Armstrong.' Smith was a nice man, but he might have warned me. Armstrong was pleasant enough, hoping that I was 'with it'. What he clearly meant was that he hoped I was without it.

The lesson was swift in coming – not via a letter on Inland Revenue paper (which would certainly have worried me) but 'just a word in my ear' to the effect that some readers might find the poetry of Roy Fuller, Vernon Watkins and Anna Akhmatova not quite what they expected. My next three issues struck Armstrong forcefully in the cerebral cortex with poems by John Heath-Stubbs, Adrian Mitchell, George Barker, Christopher Logue, Ted Hughes and finally a 23-page poem, *Ichor*, by Gavin Bantock. Seeing this in proof, Armstrong summoned a meeting of the General Council to complain and was placated only by the offer of the President of the Society, Nevill Coghill (to whom I had cannily sent a proof), to write an introduction to the poem. His suggestion that 'it is happy for us that our new Editor is a man of risks and discoveries' may not have been quite what Armstrong had hoped for.

As Muriel Spark had done before me I insisted that 'if you're a driver, you drive' – that I would publish what I liked, and that the lady who wrote from the South of France complaining that the contents of the magazine were 'sheer drivel that is an insult to the intelligence' must simply be ignored.

I clung on for five years, introducing a number of then young poets now celebrated. I can scarcely believe that I did all that work without a salary – editors of the magazine had never been paid, and I didn't learn until years later that on my appointment the Arts Council had a grant of £500 a year for the Editor, linked to £1,000 for the General Secretary – conditional on the secretary *not being Robert Armstrong*. The offer was naturally refused. I was awarded a small 'honorarium' for the last two years – less than I could have earned by writing one sixty-minute radio feature.

My memory of my time in Earls Court Square (where the offices were in my day) are by no means all unpleasant. The staff – the young women in the office ('the girls' of course, in those days) – were delightful, and almost shed a tear of sympathy when handing me every Monday the huge envelopes containing 500 or so unsolicited poems (as the only publication with the word 'poetry' in its title, the *Review* received everything from everybody).

There were some notable readings connected with the magazine – I can still see Betjeman settled cosily before the fire with his newly published copy of *High and Low*, and an equally dear man, the wonderfully sympathetic later President of the Society, William Plomer, shyly reading his hilarious poem 'The Flying Bum'. And there was the splendid 24 hours during which, in relays, a group of members read all 17 cantos of Byron's *Don Juan* to celebrate the magazine's successful campaign to have the poet commemorated in Westminster Abbey.

Since my time, *Poetry Review* has continued under a series of editors, most of them poets, and has never regressed to the state of pale amateurism from which Muriel Spark started to rescue it. I made my mistakes – one of which was perhaps to devote a whole issue to the poems of Sacheverell Sitwell. But the hoo-ha that almost prevented that issue from coming out was the last skirmish of the Battle of Earls Court Square, and for Robert Armstrong a final defeat.

Years later, in 1998, when Muriel Spark received a Golden PEN award, I offered her his posthumous congratulations. The air turned blue.

DEREK PARKER *lives in Sydney and delights in the long poems no one else now seems to read:* Idylls of the King *and* Paradise Lost *and Crabbe's marvellous* The Village. *Who, he asks, needs sonnets?*

The *Slightly Foxed* Crossword No. 10: Answers

Across: 4 THRASHER 8,10 MAGGIE TULLIVER 9 EMSWORTH 11 EDMUND 12 MESMERIC 13 HEADCASE 16 GADSHILL 19 PHAEDRIA 21 PORTIA 23 PETER PAN 24 ETHEREGE 25 UTOPIA 26 SEE 14 DOWN

Down: 1 CAPULET 2 AGE LIMITS 3 DEEVER 4 THE RACHEL PAPERS 5 RASSELAS 6 STORM 7 EXTENDS 14 AND 26 ACROSS CHODERLOS DE LACLOS 15 MIRABELL 17 APOSTLE 18 PISANIO 20 ARTHUR 22 THERA

Bibliography

Coming attractions

PIERS PLOWRIGHT confronts a burning issue · SARAH CROWDEN
takes to the by-roads in Andalusia · ANTHONY LONGDEN goes to
war with Lord Alanbrooke · URSULA BUCHAN enjoys a quiet time
at the Manse · SIMON WINDER travels a long way from Surrey ·
MICHÈLE ROBERTS is stalked by ghosts from the past · MICHAEL
LEAPMAN finds a comic novel no laughing matter · OLIVIA POTTS
spends a fruitful summer with Jane Grigson · OLIVER PRITCHETT
tries not to repeat himself

YOU'RE INVITED

THE LONDON LIBRARY

Slightly Foxed readers are invited to The London Library for a special free event on Wednesday 3 April, 6.30 p.m.

Come on a tour of this historic literary institution and view our one million books, all on open shelves. Hear our stories and find out more about our heritage and collection. Meet like-minded people and enjoy a drink in our beautiful surroundings.

Places are limited, book now londonlibrary.co.uk/reader-event